The Jesus Path

THE JESUS PATH

7 Steps to a Cosmic Awakening

Vicky Thompson

Red Wheel
Boston, MA / York Beach, ME

First published in 2003 by Red Wheel/Weiser, LLC
York Beach, ME
With offices at:
368 Congress Street, Boston, MA 02210
www.redwheelweiser.com

Library of Congress Cataloging-in-Publication Data
Thompson, Vicky.
    The Jesus path : 7 steps to a cosmic awakening / Vicky
Thompson.
        p. cm.
    ISBN 1-59003-053-2 (pbk.)
    1. Jesus Christ—New Age movement interpretations.
    2. Spiritual life—New Age movement. I. Title.
    BT304.93 .T46 2003
    232.9—dc21

                                                2002152707

Typeset in Adobe Garamond
Text design by Joyce C. Weston
Printed in Canada
TCP

10 09 08 07 06 05 04 03
8 7 6 5 4 3 2 1
The paper used in this publication meets the minimum requirements
of the American National Standard for Information Sciences—
Permanence of Paper for Printed Library Materials
Z39.48-1992 (R1997).

CONTENTS

INTRODUCTION

J E S U S walked this Earth more than two thousand years ago. A simple yet educated carpenter who became the Messiah of the people, he inspired countless generations to seek a higher way of living. He came to this Earth to demonstrate how to rise above the pain of everyday life to become a divine being having a human experience. He showed us how to simultaneously coexist in the divine and human realms by being aware of his inner greatness and using that energy to inspire peace in others and in the world. Most of all, he demonstrated that human beings can achieve wondrous things through the power of God.

A part of our growth as human beings is reconnecting with our inner spirituality and wisdom, which Jesus referred to as allowing the power of God or Spirit to work through the human creation. The universal power of God is all-encompassing, and Jesus recognized that spirit on all levels, from his own spirit-self to the Great Spirit of the universe, is a part of the whole, harmonious world of the divine. In that light, the terms "God" and "Spirit" are used interchangeably throughout the book.

Jesus' humanity makes him one of us, and his incredible ability to follow Spirit in all things despite being a part of the human condition makes him a master teacher to us. This is the heart of his example of living life in communion with Spirit.

Yet many have missed the opportunity to live the core of Jesus' teachings: He was human, just like us, and we can achieve the same commitment and strength in leading a Spirit-driven life. Scriptures in the Bible present Jesus as different, greater than mere mortals who still walk upon this Earth, but all humans can learn to reach new levels of consciousness. Just as we can try to emulate the tenets of Christ's teachings on compassion, service, and love in the Bible, we also can follow his path of spiritual transformation and walk with Spirit on a journey to our own spiritual self-awakening. We can access our inner greatness by practicing the same spiritual growth techniques that Jesus used to achieve a cosmic awakening, which is a process of allowing the universal power of God to flow through us, creating harmony and order in our often chaotic lives.

Now at this critical time in humanity's evolution, the key to a simpler life and to living just like Jesus is coming through into our world consciousness. Great prophets throughout the ages have spoken of the second coming of Christ and alluded to coming disasters and the end of the world. This apocalyptic vision of the future of humankind has been presented as the final outcome of our life's work as a collective whole. But might these visions only be a possibility presented to awaken us to outcomes we can indeed change? Within us, we each hold the power of creation to live heaven or hell upon Earth.

Which reality will we choose?

At this point in history we hold the capability to effect world destruction. We also hold the capability for world transformation on a personal and global level. Within our very being, we each hold the ability to link with our higher spirit-self, the eternal part of us that resides within the divine realm. Tapping into knowledge uniquely our own, we hold the capability to transcend pain, fear, and suffering, and bring peace to our own lives as well as to those of others by integrating the abundance of our higher spirit-self into daily life. This was the secret to Jesus' ability to link so closely with Spirit to do God's work upon Earth.

Each step in a spiritual journey is singular and begins with one individual. We each hold the capacity to explore great inner realms of spirituality and reclaim the knowledge, grace, and peace that are our divine birthright. Jesus comes to us now, two thousand years later, to fulfill a promise: *Life everlasting, life eternal is yours. Follow me, and you shall find the peace you are seeking.*

Jesus was able to transcend the mundane world of ancient Israel to fulfill his role as the Messiah of peace. He awakened, as many of us are now, to his divine purpose. He did not just step out onto the road without preparation or planning. Spirit provided him with a seven-step divine model of awakening for tapping into the inner greatness of his higher spirit-self that could transform himself and others he touched upon his journey.

Throughout this book you will read stories about the awakening of Jesus and his later work as a master among the people. These stories present Jesus as someone we may not recognize. Sometimes he is frightened, alarmed by the entry of the divine world of God into his daily life. He wonders aloud if his experiences are real. We see his inner work of transformation, including encounters with masters and angels in the inner realms of existence. From his life, we learn how, through the power of God, we can become greater than we are alone. Many generations have praised the glory of Jesus and his magnificent accomplishments, but we have overlooked the most amazing part of his being: he was human—full of fear and wonderful possibility—just like us.

Jesus is unique in that he alone is the Messiah, but his divine function is the only thing that makes him different from us. We too hold within us the ability to follow and live within the divine model of awakening for transcending to a higher level of consciousness. This divine model is a gift from God to us all. Jesus lived each step of the model, giving us a detailed roadmap to follow on our own journey to greater awareness of the workings of Spirit in our daily lives.

The information presented by Spirit in *The Jesus Path* has changed and transformed my life. Through silent communion with God, I have found that I can tap into the Christ-consciousness stream of wisdom and share messages with others. I have discovered a joy for living that did not exist before. My life prior to this time was filled with pain and confusion over sexual abuse that occurred when I was a young child. Like a wounded soldier who has tried to protect herself from further pain, I have limped through life. But a divine spark changed that silent march, and now I am living a truly amazing experience: connection with a part of me that is limitless, joyful, spirited, and truly powerful.

Turning inward through meditation and chakra-clearing visualizations, I tapped into this divine world of power and began receiving divine tools for releasing old patterns and pain in my life. The desire to change and grow is a powerful motivator for opening to the guidance of Spirit. As I journeyed deeper into the inner realms of my being, I began receiving more detailed information on how Jesus was able to transform himself into the Messiah. As to why I am the recipient of these stories, I can only say that my deep intention to change my own life made me completely open to learning from the master how to live life as God intended all humans to exist. This eternal wisdom is available to us all if we so choose it.

It has truly been a joy to write *The Jesus Path* through the loving inspiration of Jesus. The warmth and compassion of Jesus was palpable as he revealed his own awakening and the seven-step divine model of awakening to create this book. The words flowed freely and fully, and it is my hope that you too may share in the wonder and amazement of knowing the inner work of Jesus. This great being continues to share his love, energy, and compassion with others so that they too may know the electric moment of a cosmic awakening to the power and presence of God.

Hear now as Jesus welcomes you on the journey to accessing your inner wisdom:

Beloved ones, close to my heart, I gaze upon you now with great wonder. You, the journeyers and seekers of knowledge, bravely set out upon your course now to find the hidden jewels within your being. Walk with me now and relive my own journey to the heart. Know how I labored with difficulty and then with joy and ease to reach my own inner greatness. I walked this path before you to show you how to find the road home. You know that road because somewhere deep within you, you are already beside me. Take that step, beloved, into the unknown moments. Savor those moments when you remember who you truly are. See yourself as I see you: my beloved brothers and sisters.

Walking with Jesus

Over the course of the past two thousand years, many have heard the call of Jesus, and yet they have doubted his message. Through prophets in the Bible, New Testament apostles and writers, we have been touched by the messages of the divine world of God. But what has kept us from accepting them into our world and living the truth of their message in our own lives?

When God comes into our world and gives us message, it takes a leap of faith to believe that what is occurring is real. We have to believe in the unseen on many levels, including:

- ✢ God exists in our daily world.
- ✢ God cares about the outcome of our affairs in the world.
- ✢ It is possible to link with Spirit and receive divine messages.
- ✢ We all have a divine purpose and plan upon Earth.
- ✢ God will remind us of our job.

Jesus directly experienced God intervening and touching his shoulder, gently awakening him from his slumber to do his job. Let God into your life as Jesus did and feel for yourself what you need and want to do in life through the power of Spirit.

Hear now as God issues the clarion call of awakening:

Dear ones, I am calling my children to open their eyes, release the shackles from their arms, and walk freely in this beautiful world. You look down to the earth, your noses to the grindstone, and vow that one day you will have more time to do the things that you love. My call is to awaken you today. That moment of time is here for you to raise your eyes and see that the heaven you desire has been here all along, right beside you. Know that death is not the only way to return home. Your will, strength of character, and desire to break the chains of this nominal existence are like a living death of the old illusions of pain and fear. Bury the illusions and become a fully conscious and aware being here on Earth. I do not ask this of you, I tell you that this is the new coming, the new way of being on Earth. Things are changing all around you, and you must go with the tide, not fight it. Let me be your boat, for I will carry you home safely.

Come now and enter the divine world of Jesus to learn how to awaken with love to be the person whom you truly desire to be. Cast away all rigid religious views of who Jesus was and listen to this being who once lived on Earth as you do now. Get to know Jesus the man and learn from his journey home to his higher spirit-self.

1

Jesus Reveals
His Divine Awakening

"**AWAKE** and know that you are not alone," God said to me one early spring morning in Oregon when I began my own spiritual journey at the turn of the new millennium. Those words catalyzed and moved me to test the limits of my own existence. Each new experience was exciting, and my own footsteps out into the vast universe seemed to be fresh, without signs of tracks from others on the path.

But humans have been walking the spiritual path for centuries, from the mystical Sufis to Buddhists to contemporary seekers practicing an eclectic brand of spirituality. One master among them all has been Jesus, the earthly representative of the essence of God. As the divine incarnate, Jesus parted the veils of separation between heaven and Earth and ushered in a new era of peace and understanding.

As a master teacher who has experienced the joy and pain of this unique process, Jesus offers great insight on mastering the path to the higher spirit-self:

Do not shield your eyes from the divine. You exist within the divine world now, but your heart is closed to the wonders around you. The joy of rediscovering this vast dimension of peace, love, unity, and timelessness is yours now. Come with me, dear friend, on this journey and I will walk with you and greet you in your wholeness when we reunite once more. You do not need to experience death to be one with me. You only need to open your heart now to live eternally today with me.

Jesus lived during brutal times in ancient Israel. Life then was very different than our lives today. Men and women were not equal, and children had no rights and no advocates. Strict laws of purity from the Judaic tradition governed how the Jewish people could interact with others, what food they could eat, how they received their education, when they could work, and countless other aspects of daily life. The religious laws of pure living overshadowed the inner Spirit of these ancient people.

The New Testament of the Bible explains how Jesus shook up this world of entrenched convention. We see a powerful man overturning vendor tables in the temple, healing on the Jewish Sabbath, touching the impure misfits of society, and openly accepting women and lower-class people as spiritual seekers. We see Jesus as the Messiah, a man seemingly without fear or doubt, guided by the knowing hand of Spirit to do God's work upon Earth. We believe that this power and strength came solely from the grace of God, bestowed upon this being named Jesus who seemed not of this Earth. In reading these stories of Jesus' great accomplishments we forget, and sometimes even doubt, that Jesus was human, just like us.

The Jesus we read about in the Bible represents what can be achieved when you submit to God and align your will with Spirit. But how can mere mortals follow in the footsteps of the Messiah, the son of God? Can we even dare think that we can receive help abundant from Spirit just like this great master who seemed to hold favor with God? What makes us worthy to receive the same divine help as Jesus did in doing his work upon Earth?

Our understanding of this missing piece of commonality is in our very blood: Jesus was human, just like us, and his experiences reflect the great possibilities available to us all in living as an instrument of God. He is a pinnacle example of leading a Spirit-driven life, and yet he told his disciples that they could achieve all he did and more. Jesus recognized that he was not alone in achieving great things through the love of God and openly invited others to take up the charge and do God's work.

If this is true, how can we follow in the footsteps of Jesus? To believe that we too could achieve a complete connection with Spirit for guidance, wisdom, and power, we would have to accept that Jesus had our same human frailties: pain, fear, anger, anxiety, disbelief, and doubt. If Jesus began his journey as a human, how did he become a great master with mystical abilities to heal others with the touch of his hand, foresee his betrayal by his disciples, and know of his imminent death on the cross?

He started at the beginning, just as we all do, and learned through experience how to see the hand of God influencing his daily world. He opened to Spirit and was introduced to the possibility that he was not just a mere mortal living in a brutal world of death and destruction. He awakened and learned how to access his inner communication with Spirit. To become a man of God, he had to let God into his life and recognize that God was not separate from him, but within and without him. He had to say, "Yes, God, I will do your work upon Earth, knowing that you are all upon this Earth." He had to be God's instrument, just as we can too in our own unique way.

When you open to the possibility that you are more than just a physical body, you become aware that God works through you. You begin to see the subtle work of Spirit in our lives, and how it influences what we create. Great inspirations, seemingly effortless to achieve, come to us when we open our minds and call upon the greater force of the universe to manifest our dreams. We hold the choice of free will as God's creations, and one of the greatest choices you can make is to accept God's will as your own. Jesus showed us that amazing miracles can occur when you rely upon a power greater than your own. We know that Jesus will always be the Messiah, a master teacher with great courage, love, compassion, and faith. But what will we achieve by aligning our will with God's and connecting with our own divine plan? What great things will you do to further God's work upon Earth? Do you believe that God will provide the same abundance he did for Jesus to help you fulfill an important divine function upon Earth too?

Belief also was a part of the beginning of Jesus' journey to knowing the God within.

A Spirit among Us

Jesus was born the son of a carpenter more than two thousand years ago. He lived a simple life and followed in the footsteps of his father, Joseph, until his early twenties. Throughout his youth, he felt an awareness of something greater within him. An understanding of life and people's complicated emotions always seemed to be within his grasp. He was aware of himself as a spiritual being, but on a different level than the temple and its teachings. From his early education, he knew the Hebrew Bible well and understood its lessons, but he took it a step further by combining his spiritual awareness with his Bible knowledge. This made him feel that on some level he was a part of all things in the world. He saw the interrelationship between humans and nature, God and humans, and God and nature. He saw them all as a part of the great universe of God, a wondrous place of unity and discord, harmony and hatred, suffering and abundance, and life and death. He saw himself within this universe of God and felt that he had some important role to play, but he did not know what. He was aware of the kingdom of God, but his awakening to his spiritual purpose had not yet come.

A spiritual awakening begins when you make a choice to align your will with God's will. All it takes is a breath, a small indication, to let God know that you are ready to begin your chosen role upon Earth. Give an inch to Spirit, and God will take you a mile upon your journey. All spiritual awakenings are similar in four ways. To experience the journey of awakening, you need to do the following:

✛ Let Spirit know that you are ready to begin the journey to performing your divine function upon Earth. Prayer, meditation, statements of intention, and other indicators can be used to let God know that you have made a conscious choice to be greater than you are alone.

✛ Begin an energetic process of releasing old illusions in your life, including pain, fear, anger, and other patterns of behavior that don't serve you well. The release process is done on a conscious and unconsciousness level with the help of Spirit through prayer, dream work, meditation, affirmations, and experiences that help you to recognize old energy that you need to let go.

✛ Welcome divine guidance and inner wisdom into your conscious mind. As you go through the release process, you will open your awareness to the divine world in daily life. Pulling from a greater source of power for living, you can tap into this wisdom through your intuitive senses of seeing, hearing, knowing, and feeling.

✛ Integrate your divine experiences into your daily life. As you connect into your eternal essence, you will begin to view the world in a new way. These new insights need to be assimilated into your new worldview. You'll begin to perceive life as fuller, richer in growth opportunities to know yourself and others in their true state of mastery.

Jesus began to feel restless in his early twenties, ready for a spiritual change in his life. He increasingly felt that he was missing something, that he had forgotten some important thing that he needed to do. He sought out a quiet place in the hills near his house to pray to God for guidance on what to do with his life. He opened the door to God in a simple way and God responded.

The revelation of his divine role came shortly after. Jesus began having powerful dreams at night. The dreams continued over the course of a week, building in intensity until one night the doors of heaven opened and revealed his destiny upon Earth.

In the dream, he was visited by an angel who wore a crown of flowers. She told Jesus that the Lord was within him and a fire would awaken his heart. Feeling a physical sensation of burning in his chest, Jesus looked down and saw a violet flame burning within his heart. He watched as it expanded through his being and out into four oval-shaped energy fields that surrounded his body. These fields grew larger until they all united as one powerful field around his body.

Still dreaming, he experienced a shift in awareness that enabled him to see his entire body as if he were standing in front of himself. He saw seven balls of color stacked upon each other from the base of his spine to the top of his head: red, orange, yellow, green, blue, indigo, and purple. He gazed in wonder as these balls took on an inner luminosity. Suddenly a bolt of white lightning struck his head, and he could feel it opening to receive tremendous energy. His body shook as the light streamed into his being. Suddenly the balls opened, creating a column to hold the white energy in his body.

In the dream, he looked up in wonder as another angel appeared at his side. This huge, powerful angel placed his hands upon Jesus' head and heart.

"Let there be light in your heart," said the angel. "Know that you are one with the divine. The light of God shines through your being. You are the hope of the world, the one who they call Messiah. You are the messenger, you are the living message. You are the peace-giver, you are the peace. You are the lover, you are love. You are the Messiah, the one they call the son of God. You are God, you are the bringer of light. Awake now and go forth with your message of love."

Jesus awoke from the dream with a start. His clothes were soaked with sweat and he wiped the water from his brow. His chest was burning, just as in the dream. His whole body was tingling, like some hidden power was coursing through his being. His stood up and shook his arms and legs. He felt full of energy and yet weak at the same time.

Suddenly a ball of white light exploded into the room, like a star bursting forth into the heavens. Jesus let out a small cry as he jumped back from the light.

"Fear not, dear one," said a voice by Jesus' ear.

Jesus spun around to see who was standing by him, but no one was there.

"Look into the light and I will be revealed," said the voice.

Jesus turned back to the ball of white light. Startled, he jumped back again. Before him stood his guardian angel, the one who wore the flower crown in his dream.

"Lord, am I awake?" he asked out loud.

"Yes, you are awake and you have awoken, as God has commanded you," the angel said.

Jesus fell to his knees. His heart felt like it was on fire and tears streamed from his eyes as he looked upon the angel.

"Angel of God, is it true that I am the one they will call the Messiah?" he asked the shimmering being in front of him.

"Rejoice and open your heart, for your time to awaken and be the messenger of God is here. You will lead the people of Israel to peace within," the angel replied. "You are the Messiah."

Jesus lay on the ground as sobs tore through his body. He felt joy as well as fear about what lay ahead.

"Fear not, dear one," said the angel. "God is within you and will guide you every step of the way. You are a representative of a whole host of divine beings who will help you to bring a message of peace and love to Israel and to the world."

As Jesus raised his head, the being disappeared in a flash of light. But the voice of the angel continued to whisper in his ear, "I am always here with you, dear one. Only think of me and I will answer."

Jesus lay back down and felt a calming energy flow through his body. He returned to sleep and did not dream again that night.

The True Essence of God

Jesus the man learned that he could become Jesus the Messiah in a glorious moment of awakening. His heart opened to the power and energy of God, and he was forever changed. He no longer could view his earthly life as the definition of his existence. The world of God had entered his life, and it would never be the same again.

As a human being who has lived on Earth, Jesus knows what it is like to feel fear, betrayal, and scarcity. He also knows what it is like to rise above these illusions to enter into the kingdom of heaven while still living here upon Earth. But to attain that mastery, you have to go through the process of awakening to your inner greatness.

An awakening holds many moments and opportunities for mastery. Jesus experienced a divine connection through his unconscious mind during a dream state. The divine often connects with us on this dream level while our conscious mind is at rest, allowing guidance and inspiration to enter our realm of possibilities. When Jesus awoke from the dream, his divine experience continued and his conscious awareness was engaged. This dramatic encounter with his guardian angel was the consciousness opening point on his journey to becoming the Messiah. The moment the unconscious becomes a part of your conscious awareness, the hand of God can reach into your world and change your life. The divine dream becomes a reality and can shift our perception of the world from purely physical to a spiritual realm of possibilities.

As Jesus' experience shows, we don't awaken spiritually in a state of mastery. We take steps and go through experiences to learn firsthand how to remember our inner greatness. We experience a connection with a source of power greater than our own. We connect with the divine, the world of God, and begin the process of breaking down barriers to the truth of our existence and our eternal connection with God. We remember that we are not separate from God but a part of God. In shattering the illusion of separation, we learn to pull from this abundant power and find ways to live as instruments of God upon Earth. During Jesus' journey, he began to realize that his existence was limitless and eternal. This knowledge freed him from living a life of convention and allowed him to step out and lead a faith revolution and, ultimately, the world.

Deep within us all exists a divine being, a higher spirit-self of whom we are unaware. Within our mind and body dwell higher levels of awareness and consciousness. This elevated consciousness is accessed through opening our divine channels of intuitive communication with our eternal essence. By expanding our awareness of the totality of our being, we begin to recognize that we are energetically greater than the physical human body that we identify as ourselves. Energetically, we are the pure light of God, a powerful stream of energy that extends from our divine higher spirit-self into this human form. In our experience of life on Earth, we have forgotten our own inner abundance and connection with God. A spiritual awakening is a glorious process of remembering our cosmic link with the universal world of God.

Jesus awoke to be the Messiah, a critical messenger needed

two thousand years ago as well as today. You also will awaken to your higher spirit-self, a being residing with God and holding all knowledge of this universe. Just as Jesus was needed to lead the world back to God, you are needed to perform an important divine function. Nurturer, caregiver, leader, scholar, scientist, illuminator, healer, messenger, creator—all of these functions are needed to move the world forward into a new age of peace.

In this moment, you may feel like you have the potential for greatness within, but you don't know how to reveal it. We all hold the essence of God within, and like Jesus, we too can shed the illusions of fear that keep us bound to a limited existence. The courage to try something new and frightening was not something that God only gave to Jesus. You hold the same power within you to unlock the greatness of your higher spirit-self and serve others like Jesus did upon his path to mastery.

The words of Jesus catalyzed an ancient nation to seek greatness and new religions to grow in support of his teachings. But during the two thousand years since his physical death, people and religions have moved away from the true essence of his tenets of love, peace, and harmony. We have forgotten why the master came to lead us. Instead, we have gotten caught up in leading our daily lives and in exerting the physical, emotional, and mental energy required to run a family, our business, and the world. Our inner spirituality is asking us to stop running and take a moment to hear with fresh ears what Jesus has to say to us about the meaning of life. That's what a spiritual awakening is about: shifting from an outer focus to receive our inner wisdom.

Jesus' teachings on shifting this spiritual focus were simple and yet profound:

> Love yourself as you would God, for you are a part of God. You hold seeds of greatness within, hungering for the light of God to encourage them to grow. Let your divinity shine through, and know that heaven is not above you but within you. Look within to God, and you will know how to treat your neighbors: treat them as God. Have the strength to believe in my words, for they are your words too. We come from the same divine source of love that created humans and this universe too.

Jesus awoke to begin the world's journey back home to the divine within. He, like many of the great masters who achieved total communion with God while upon Earth, was a living example of a path to follow. He has left many keys for us to find, many notes for us to read, and many fruits for us to nourish ourselves upon our own journey. We only need the same courage to try something new and take the first step toward remembering our divinity. Today, Jesus continues his work of bringing the good news of God to all people throughout the world. For the good news is that God loves you and is ready to help you to awaken and remember who you are: a divine being who has momentarily forgotten his or her inner greatness. And like Jesus, you are a beloved child of God, and you can receive help abundant in this process of remembering how to see heaven upon Earth.

This is your choice: to live a life of separation on Earth or to live heaven upon Earth. Will you awaken and discern which reality will lead you back to the heart of God?

The first choice is to follow the reality of the seemingly separate physical world we live in. When we buy into the illusions of a life of separation from Spirit, pitfalls of perception can cloud our vision of the world. On Earth, we have separate nations with mainly separate economies, cultures, and beliefs. We separate ourselves from others based on the color of our skin, income, social circles, religion, gender, education, regions, and many other factors. This world is based upon differences that divide, and where none exist, we oftentimes create the division. Pain, suffering, fear, destitution, anger, hatred, and bigotry are emotions and states of mind that we all seem to fight against. This life of separation from God can become hell on Earth.

This separation from our inherent divinity has created great pain in our lives. When Jesus experienced his dream of awakening, he had to contend with his own fears of becoming the Messiah. Prophets were not revered by the Jewish temple leaders or the Romans in ancient Israel, so Jesus knew that on his path he would endure ridicule, hatred, and pain. And yet he felt the power of God through the angelic beings that awoke him to his destiny. He felt that through the grace and loving help of God, he could be whatever God wanted him to be.

The second choice is to awaken to a reality that currently exists beyond our level of comprehension. This hidden world of the divine does not just exist above you in the celestial realm. It exists beside you, above you, below you, and inside of you, but on a different level of perception. As humans, we have the capacity to evolve and change, using dormant intuitive functions in our bodies that we did not know were available for our spiritual growth.

We have discovered many mysteries of the universe, and this knowledge has left us with the belief that we know it all and only science can prove it to us otherwise. Our reliance on the empirical will hamper our journey into this new reality of the divine on Earth. But since this divine reality keeps surfacing, perhaps now is the time to lay aside the inner skeptic and muster the courage to explore this uncharted territory of the mind and soul.

The Journey to Awakening

Just as Jesus awoke to his mission, you will awake to your mission too. It may seem presumptuous to say that you have a mission here when you may not even be aware of it yourself, but the divine reality is that we are more than just humans living and dying on Earth. We all have higher spirit-selves that reside in the divine realm, which coexists with us here on Earth. But our conscious awareness of the divine realm is blocked by pain and fear. These feelings cause us to believe that we are separate from God and all others on Earth and prevent us from seeing the divine realm on Earth. The earthly experience has often been described as a school for mastering the feelings of separation from God and reconnecting with our eternal source.

Feelings of separation are no more than blocks in our body's energetic system. The human body is surrounded by four oval-shaped energy fields: the physical, emotional, mental, and spiritual fields. These fields interact directly with the human body's chakra energy system, which are the seven energy sites located in the trunk and head of the body. The chakras have specific colors, functions, and energies that affect the body and its energy fields.

This hidden function of the human body is purely divine in nature: chakras and energy fields act as communication receivers

THE DIVINE CONNECTION:
The Human Energetic System

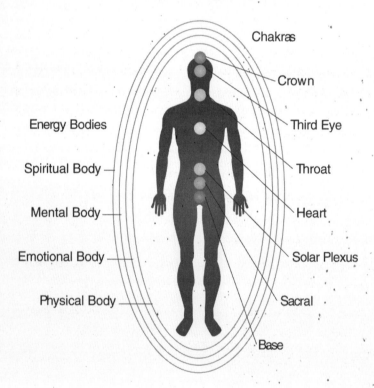

Chakras
Crown
Third Eye
Throat
Heart
Solar Plexus
Sacral
Base

Energy Bodies
Spiritual Body
Mental Body
Emotional Body
Physical Body

with the divine realm. By clearing out blocked chakras and energy fields, you can open up your intuitive senses of hearing, seeing, knowing, and feeling, and increase your awareness of the divine world around you. The divine realm consists of pure light energy, and your chakras and energy fields interact with this divine light and interpret the guidance coming into your conscious awareness. Your energetic system acts like a foreign language interpreter: it takes the limitless energy input from God and translates it into understandable language and guidance, which is then fed in through your intuitive senses so that you can receive the communication. Clear chakras and energy fields are vital to receiving clear communication from the divine.

In most people, the chakras are blocked, meaning old issues, fears, and emotions cloud these translucent balls of energy. A closed chakra system limits the awareness of the divine realm because the chakras are unable to exchange energetic information with the four energy fields. The body becomes like a

Chakra	Location	Color	Function
Base	Base of the spine	Red	Security, survival
Sacral	Midway between navel and base of spine	Orange	Sexuality, creativity
Solar Plexus	Behind navel	Yellow	Power, control
Heart	Chest	Green	Love
Throat	Behind Adam's apple	Blue	Communication
Third Eye	Middle of forehead	Indigo	Divine vision
Crown	Top of head	Purple	Divine knowledge

computer with a missing circuit. Power cannot move completely through the system, so information input and output is blocked. The mind and body become closed to divine guidance, and feelings of separation are intensified. Clearing the chakras and energy fields of old pain, fear, anger, and other blocking energies opens up the link of communication with our inner spiritual wisdom.

Jesus first experienced this process during his dream when his chakras were cleared by angelic beings while he slept. When this process was complete, Jesus' awareness of the divine realm on Earth began to open. He awoke from the dream and connected with his guardian angel to begin the journey of awakening, which is a conscious process of realigning with the essence of the higher spirit-self. With a clear, open energetic system, Jesus became conscious of the divine intervention in his life and aware of the guidance flowing into his receivers. This consciousness allowed him to later receive training from divine masters and begin the work of removing his illusions of separation from God.

If you desire a Spirit-driven life, cleaning out your energetic system will prepare you for an open connection with your inner wisdom and power. Jesus initially received divine help in clearing his energy system, so that later on he could learn how to do his own consciousness clearing. Chakra and energy field clearing can be done through simple meditations and visualizations, or with the help of Spirit.

Clearing your energetic system of blocking energy is done through the power of intention, and the strength of your desire to connect with your inner wisdom will determine how quickly you move forward. In chakra-clearing visualizations, what you see is generally what you get. If you begin to see and accept that you are whole and full of God's abundance, your energetic system will respond and create that divine reality in your life. Take a moment now to experience the power of opening your energetic system on your own. The following visualization will lead you through a simple method for clearing your chakras and energy fields. In keeping it simple, don't worry about seeing the chakras in exactly the right spot in the body or how big they should appear. Hold in your mind the thought that you are whole and complete right in this moment, and that you are choosing to actualize that divine state now in your human body. In this state of wholeness, all that you experience in the visualization is just right for you in this moment.

Divine Connection Visualization

Close your eyes and take some slow, deep breaths. See your body as if you were standing in front of yourself. Visualize a stack of seven balls inside your body, from the base of your spine extending up to the crown of your head. Starting at the bottom of the stack, see a red ball, full and glowing. Move your attention up to the next ball and see this orange orb as full and alive. Now move up through the rest of the balls and see them as clear and glowing. Yellow, green, blue, indigo, and purple, up to the top of your head. Now see a white light pouring down into your crown, filling your body up, starting at the toes, rushing up the legs, torso, spilling into the arms, up the neck, and filling the head. The light is so intense that it continues to flow out of your crown and quickly fills the four energy fields encircling your body. See yourself as glowing, vibrant, and full of light and love. Gently open your eyes, knowing that you are full of divine abundance and life everlasting.

All you need is within you, and God will supply the rest. These energy systems currently exist in all people. All you need to do is align your intention with God's will and plan for you, and you will receive help abundant in opening and beginning this process. As you begin your journey home to the higher spirit-self, you will learn what your mission is and how the divine will help you to best prepare for it. Jesus was given what he needed to perform his divine function, just as you will be provided with all of the divine help you need to be an instrument of God.

Know Me As You Know Yourself

Jesus spoke of love for others, God, and self. He embodied the true meaning of the word "love": an ability to open fully to the elements of another being and appreciate that individual's essence. Love has taken on many meanings in our world, but in the divine sense, love is about feeling, knowing, and sensing what is germane to a person's core being. We all come from God, and we all contain his essence of love within. Beyond that great gift, we each have elements that are uniquely expressed. Some may express incredible artistic talent, others may have scientific minds, others may be leaders, some may be nurturers of the soul, and some may be adventurers on the road of life.

We each take our God essence and transform that energy to uniquely express our own journeys on Earth, and like astronauts in space linked to ground control, we feed this information back to God. This unified source of all beings assimilates all experiences into one stream of consciousness. This source further evolves and grows as more is learned about all elements of life. This universal consciousness supports all life abundantly, supplying our world with love, hope, faith, peace, compassion, and wisdom. This energy is available to us all on Earth if we so choose to accept and open ourselves to the flow of heaven's abundance. If one thing could be said about the difference between heaven and Earth, it would simply be "experience." We experience many things during our lives here, and each moment is an opportunity to grow, learn, and change. What are we growing, learning, and changing toward? God, and the remembrance of our inner connection with this universal source of great love.

The story of Jesus' journey on Earth reminds us that we are linked with this God source of energy. He spoke of God as light and heaven as another realm or dimension of being. He showed people how to use energy to heal the body and mind and transcend the everyday world. He was a living example of remembrance, and he learned through his own experiences how to connect back to the heart of God.

Jesus went through his own awakening process to fully step into the role of the Messiah. During his dream, the divine helped with the initial opening of his chakra energy system, but that was just the first step in the energetic release process. He had old energy blocking his awareness of the divine world and his own inner greatness, and he needed to learn how to release that energy. Jesus began communicating with his guardian angel to remember how to use the abilities of his higher spirit-self and continue the conscious energy release process.

A few days after the dream, Jesus was walking by a river. He felt troubled by this new path he was embarking upon. He wondered if he had the strength to do what God was asking of him. He walked down the bank of the river, removed his sandals, and stood in the water.

He looked up to see a bird flying over the water. It landed on a log stuck near the shore. For a long time, the bird stared at him. Suddenly the bird took off into the air, flying straight toward Jesus.

As he was lifting his arms to shield his face, Jesus heard a voice beside him say, "Fear not, for you have looked into the eyes of God."

Jesus lowered his arms to his sides. The bird flew toward him and gently landed on his shoulder.

"Angel, you are with me again," he spoke aloud. The bird sat quietly as Jesus looked at it out of the corner of his eye.

"Know me as you know yourself," a new voice said.

Instantly, Jesus knew that the voice of God was speaking from within him. He felt a great burning in his chest, like his heart was spinning and opening wider. The claws of the bird, sharp upon his skin, held him steady against the great stirring within his body.

For an instant, he felt himself become a part of the bird. He could see himself through the bird's eyes. A pinkish glow surrounded his body and a stream of white light flowed into the top of his head. Just as quickly as this awareness had come, it was gone.

Jesus was back within himself, but he didn't feel the same.

"I feel you within me, my God, and I know you as my creator, my beloved," he said, tears streaming down his cheeks.

From deep within Jesus' being, God said, "My beloved, my joy in speaking with you is uncontainable. My dear one, my one of the heart, I have awakened a fire within you so that you may lead your brothers and sisters home to me."

"Welcome . . . welcome . . . welcome," a soft voice next to Jesus whispered. He turned his head to see the bird alight from his shoulder and fly into the sun.

The Master within Us All

The journey back to God is not solitary. One of the first steps in reconnecting with Spirit is realizing that you are dependent upon God. It may sound contradictory that you are dependent upon God when you may feel separate from God, but recognizing that God is truly running the show of the universe will change how you view yourself and your chosen role in this great drama. In being dependent upon God, you realize that your true power does not come from your own labor, your own ideas, or your own free will in life. True power flows from God, who helps you manifest your divine plan with ease, abundance, and love. In remembering that you can pull from a power greater than your own limited resources, you align your will with Spirit and become a master like Jesus in planting the seeds of God's greatness in the earthly experience. Dependence on God actually becomes you, of your own free will, choosing to act as an agent of spiritual change in the world for the love of God.

The first step in aligning with the will of Spirit is accepting that divine beings work in concert, and you too have a part to play in the symphony. Connecting with our higher spirit-self is a part of God's plan for us all. Just as Jesus had God and many angels and masters assisting him in his divine work, you too can receive divine help to open your connection with your higher spirit-self. This higher spirit-self is linked to you energetically, but your awareness of your divine self may be blocked by old issues and pain that have closed down your chakra and energy field systems.

It may seem strange to think that you have other dimensions of self of which you are unaware. Many of us feel that we are the masters of the show here, and the possibility that we are anything more than this flesh-and-blood body is unbelievable. And if we really do have a higher spirit-self, why are we in a crummy job, a bad relationship, or financial straits? Wouldn't our higher spirit-self want us to live a life without strife?

As a former Catholic who was sexually abused as a child, I have wondered about this. If we align our will with Spirit and make God's plan our own, then it follows that we all choose our lives here on Earth, and that each experience is a chance to grow and learn more about ourselves and to reconnect with the God of our hearts. We act as physical extensions of our higher spirit-self, and we live out our plan with God upon Earth. We choose to be born into this world into a particular family to gain a valuable life experience. But I have had a hard time reconciling that view with the idea that I would choose to be sexually abused. Why would I ask to be hurt and humiliated?

Jesus came to me one afternoon as I was pondering this idea that I am a masochist. I felt a tingling in my upper back as I sensed Jesus' hand come to rest between my shoulders.

"Dear one, to understand why we choose certain life experiences, you need to turn your perspective from outside to inside," he said to my inner ears. "In an outside perspective on Earth, you look out to others who tell you that it was not your fault that you were abused, that you played no part in it, and it is solely the responsibility of your grandfather."

"Which is true," I interrupted.

"Yes, it is true in the sense of the abuse experience that occurred," he replied. "For you on Earth, it seems like it was a terrible, unavoidable experience over which you had no control. You may even go so far as to rage against God for the injustice of it all. You feel alone, helpless, and powerless in this outside perspective.

"But when you shift your perspective from looking outside yourself to looking inside yourself, you can understand why we choose certain experiences on Earth. You chose to come into a situation of abuse because you wanted to learn how you would react and grow in that situation. Divine beings are inquisitive by nature and wish to challenge themselves. In the divine realm, there is no separation from God, so we are not faced with fears, scarcity, or lack of any kind. We are all linked energetically, so there is no possibility of duplicity or hiding the truth. We create earthly realms so that we may explore who we are in every experience."

Jesus paused to allow me to think about what he said.

I felt angry and confused. I had never considered that I had any choice about the abuse. I had only seen myself as powerless, unable to stop my grandfather. I took slow, deep breaths until the emotional wave passed and I could explore what Jesus had said.

Finally, I replied, "So looking from the inside perspective, I chose this life to learn more about myself through experiences in which I am unable to use my power of choice to stop someone from hurting me. Inside, I still hold the power of choice to end now what I couldn't stop my grandfather from doing then. I can choose today to let go of the pain of the past, and not let it rule my life."

"Yes, you wanted to find out if you could overcome the pain and fear that was instilled in you from the abuse," Jesus said. "You wanted to know if you could release all of that energy and reconnect with God. By going through this experience, you would return stronger, knowing that you could sink to the depths, but still receive the grace and love of God to carry you home. You wanted to be an everyday hero within the sight of God."

In choosing to follow the will of God, we recognize that there is a knowing, wise part of us that has carefully planned our journey here upon Earth. If one of the goals of life is remembering our inner connection with the eternal aspect of our Spirit, then each experience becomes an opportunity to choose to make this connection. Each trial and tribulation becomes a moment for personal greatness and a chance to pull from the greater resource of Spirit. My own pain over my childhood abuse compelled me to seek help from a power greater than my own. That experience catalyzed growth despite the pain I endured. We each can choose how we view our life's experiences: as a mortal blow to living a full life or as a gift that we must open and explore and accept in our life. A gift offers us the chance to see every experience as an opportunity, full of pain, revelation, and joy. Life is rich, and we can choose to be a part of its abundance.

In choosing abundance, we choose to live as God intended.

2

Using the Divine Model of Awakening in Daily Life

AS JESUS experienced more divine encounters that further opened him to the divine world and his own power, he received a prescription for living as a divine being in human form. As the human representative of God on Earth, Jesus needed to shed his old pretenses and way of life to become the Messiah, a human capable of leading others to the divine within. Jesus needed to release old issues from his life that had become habits used to distance himself from others.

All of us carry around old war wounds from experiences and incidents with others. Our parents shape our early lives and leave us with tears of sadness as well as happiness. We learn within our family system how to survive in the world. Based upon our survival experiences, we may either turn off or enhance our ability to love, have compassion for others, develop strength of character, and express humility. These four personality traits influence how we interact with others in the world.

Love, compassion, strength of character, and humility act as points on a barometer gauging our level of functioning in the world. Divine beings hold these four personality traits at high, even levels. In humans, however, these traits are expressed on a lower level on the barometer based on our early experiences in life. Compared to our high-level divine counterparts, most people express these traits at a mid to low level of functioning, with the mid-level representing the greatest point of functioning most people attain. Part of the goal of a spiritual awakening is to realign these traits at the level of the higher spirit-self, opening up the ability to live life on a higher, more fulfilling spiritual level. Jesus' whole journey focused on developing these four traits to their fullest level so that he could radiate the love of God from his being to touch and change the lives of others.

Part of the realignment process involves understanding our current levels of the traits of love, compassion, strength of character, and humility. Knowing your base point will help you to identify old issues blocking your spiritual connection and realign with your higher spirit-self's trait levels.

Assessing Your Trait Levels

Rate the following statements using a scale between one and ten, where one is low and ten is high on a scale of intensity of agreement with the statement.

_____ 1. I love other people for who they are, despite their frailties or hang-ups.

_____ 2. I can accept and support other people even when I don't agree with their choices.

_____ 3. I can love other people whether or not they provide something I need.

_____ 4. When I see other people in pain, I can identify with their situations and relate them to similar experiences I have gone through.

_____ 5. When other people hurt me in some way, I can identify with their intentions and motives and relate them to similar experiences when I have also caused pain in others.

_____ 6. When I see other people in pain, I feel empathy for their experience and use the situation to grow more compassion in myself.

_____ 7. When I am faced with a challenging situation, I look inside myself and trust that I will do my best in any moment.

_____ 8. When I see other people behaving in a questionable manner, I follow my own inner code and choose my own course of action.

_____ 9. When other people hurt me, I trust myself to react in a manner that respects all involved in the situation.

_____ 10. When I am on a team, I make sure that all people receive recognition for their contributions, no matter how big or small.

_____ 11. When other people compliment me, I accept their words and simply say, "Thank you."

_____ 12. When I am on a team, I let other people make contributions without judging them.

Trait-Level Scoring: Add up your score for each set of statements and divide it by three to determine your trait levels.

TRAIT LEVEL

Score for statements 1–3 ___ ÷ 3 = ___ Love

Score for statements 4–6 ___ ÷ 3 = ___ Compassion

Score for statements 7–9 ___ ÷ 3 = ___ Strength of character

Score for statements 10–12 ___ ÷ 3 = ___ Humility

Your score gives you a general idea of areas that you will need to focus on when releasing old energy patterns. In subsequent chapters, you will do meditations and other exercises to let go of pain in your life, and knowing your trait levels will help in tailoring each tool to suit your needs. To understand how these levels affect our daily interactions, you need to look honestly at each of your personality traits and their effect on your thoughts, feelings, and actions.

Love

When we have never learned how to love another person, we may objectify people and not take responsibility for our own actions. We learn to show love to others in the world by experiencing our parents' expression of love toward us and watching them interact with other people. At the extreme, people who commit violent crimes against other beings do not comprehend that humans are living, breathing expressions of God. Instead, they may objectify people and place them in categories of "acceptable" or "expendable." However, in general, people categorize others based upon their perception of them as worthy of love. Love came at a price for most people in childhood, and we may see it as a bargaining chip, a reward, or an elusive dream. We can feel love, but we don't always know the true depth of the love experience and the pureness of the emotion. Some may confuse it with sexual expression, and others may totally separate the two. In general, most people know love on a limited level and may use it to manipulate others in gaining what they need. At other times, love may shine through, illuminating life as a glorious journey, as well as pointing out the need for a purer love connection with Spirit.

Compassion

When we do not learn to show compassion, we may become hardened to the pain in the world around us and turn our back on others. Compassion is the ability to feel empathy for others, knowing at some level that their experiences are not foreign, but ones that you can identify with without judgment. Mother Teresa is an example of a person with an evolved level of compassion. She reached out to others with love and care, but never with pity. She helped others to stand up when they may not have believed that they could. In most people, compassion is expressed through sympathy, when we feel badly for the situation of the other person, while hoping we will not have to experience the same thing. Sympathy can fall short of compassion when we don't recognize that all experiences are universal. When we do, we can grow from another's pain into higher levels of compassion within ourselves.

Strength of Character

When we have not developed strength of character, we become smaller than we really are and feel like there must be something more to this life and the role we play in it. Strength of character often is related to the level of mastery we feel in our life. Children who are told that they are not good enough, or not allowed to learn through their own efforts, show a low strength of character. In my family, my love for my mother was never good enough to change how she perceived me. I was seen as a perfectionist who did not accept her limitations, so I learned to appear less threatening to her in an attempt to win her love. My strength of character was compromised because my self-worth was tied up in gaining her approval. Many people do not develop a high strength of character because certain family dynamics or experiences limit their ability to achieve self-mastery.

Humility

When we do not learn how to express humility, we may either show false humility or none at all, which leads us to behave either in a subservient manner or to dominate others. The expression of humility depends on the level of the other three personality traits. A person who can love and be compassionate but lacks strength of character will express humility as subservience. At the opposite end, a person who doesn't know love or compassion but has a high strength of character will express false humility and dominate others. Genuine humility means showing respect and recognition for the mastery of others as well as for the self. On his journey, Jesus learned to express humility in a genuine way based on his inner work to realign with his higher spirit-self's greater levels of love, compassion, strength of character, and humility.

These personality traits were issues for Jesus as well, and he had to understand them in order to shift to a higher level of functioning. While raised by loving parents with good intentions, Jesus was a part of a human family working to survive in an often hostile environment. Joseph and Mary were not asked to shield Jesus from the world, and they needed his able hands to help with everyday life in a primitive society. Mary was not asked to treat Jesus differently from her other children, so sibling rivalries and family dynamics were a part of his childhood. Jesus was a typical young man in Roman times: hardworking and capable.

But he was unique in that he had powerful beliefs about love and an incredible strength of character. These traits helped him to awaken and answer his inner call to action. However, the inner work was just beginning on his journey to becoming a full-functioning Messiah. Working with divine masters, Jesus would learn to realign his personality traits with his higher spirit-self.

During Jesus' awakening, he had to remember how to see heaven on Earth. When we come to Earth, we don't remember our inner connection with God, and each experience becomes an opportunity to open to Spirit. Our road to remembrance can be bumpy when we carry limited personality traits, because it's harder to trust that a world of greater abundance exists beyond the earthly world we perceive in front of us. We need to have faith that we are greater than our limitations, our circumstances, our pain. Jesus learned these lessons as he began to journey deeper into connection with Spirit.

Soon after Jesus' divine encounters began, he fell asleep under a tree outside of a village. He had been working all day and felt tired. As the limbs of the tree gently swayed and fanned him, he felt a great lulling in his body. His limbs felt like they were moving with the tree, and a lightness of being lifted his spirit. He began to dream, but he felt like he was still awake. In the distance, he saw a man walking toward him. As he neared, Jesus could see that he was actually floating slightly above the ground as he moved his legs. A soft glowing light shone around the man, and Jesus felt comforted as this being placed a hand upon his arm.

"It is time," said the man.

"Who are you?" asked Jesus.

"You may call me the Old Master," he said. "We have spent many a lifetime together. Come," the Old Master said, as he gently pulled Jesus to his feet. Linking his arm through Jesus', they began to ascend to the heavens.

Time disappeared as a whirl of colors clouded Jesus' vision. When the kaleidoscope stopped turning, Jesus found himself in a small courtyard by a stream. The air felt cool and clean, and he longed to feel the water on his skin.

"Come then," said the Old Master as he led Jesus to the stream.

Kneeling down, Jesus placed his hands in the water. Feeling the pleasure of the smooth clear water running across his skin, he cupped his hands and splashed the flowing coolness on his face. But when he opened his eyes, he was no longer in the courtyard. He was alone under the tree outside the village. Dirt covered his hands and face.

In confusion, he looked around, trying to discern if he was awake.

"Angel of God, please come to me now," he said aloud.

The wind began blowing and he felt something brush his shoulder. He turned around, but only the tree was there. He walked around the tree, looking up in its branches for a sign of the angel. The wind started blowing again, and he felt a tapping on his shoulder. He spun around only to be poked in the cheek by a tree limb.

He yelled out in pain, kicking the tree trunk.

A voice whispered in his ear, "Do you not know that I am the tree?"

He turned and an angel with a crown of flowers stood before him by the tree. Her magnificent wings were fully open and a golden light shone about her.

"Pray dear angel, I did not mean to hurt you. Please forgive me," said Jesus, falling to his knees.

"There is nothing to forgive, for I do not remember what you did," replied the angel.

Jesus stared in confusion at the angel as he slowly sat down on the ground.

"I kicked the tree, which I thought you said was you, and I

say now that I am sorry," Jesus said, clearly doubting that he was awake.

"You are awake, dear one," said the angel.

Startled, he asked, "How do you know what I am thinking?"

The angel did not speak aloud, but a voice in his head said, "For we are one. I know your heart's desires, your pains, and your burdens. These loads are heavy, and I am here to help you set them down."

He looked at the smiling angel in amazement as she only nodded her head.

In this story, Jesus was shown through experience that he needed to overcome his limited perceptions and remember that heaven exists in tandem with the earthly world. With the help of a divine master, Jesus connected unconsciously into the inner realms of Spirit and then awoke to experience consciously the divine presence in the earthly world. Jesus was taken to a heavenly place where he felt the divinely cool water upon his face, only to open his eyes covered in dirt. He called to his guardian angel for help, only to end up thinking that he'd hurt her. He was stunned that she seems to have a problem with her short-term memory and even more shaken that she could hear his thoughts and communicate with him without the spoken word. In every step, he sees the earthly world: the dirt on his body, the pain he has caused another being, the confusion of forgiveness, and the fear of being found unworthy based on his inner thoughts. What he does not yet see is the divine world existing in tandem with the earthly world: the sensation of pleasure from the water, the existence of the divine in every living thing on

Earth, the total redemption of complete forgiveness, and a communion of Spirit in truthful communication.

Each step in an awakening brings us closer to knowing the truth of our existence on Earth and God's influence in our daily world.

The Divine Model of Awakening

There is a method to the journey of awakening, and as Jesus experienced more connections with Spirit, he began to receive guidance for going deeper into the depths of his being. Guidance may be detailed prescriptions for realigning aspects of personality with the higher spirit-self, or experiences designed to help the journeyer figure out the mystery of reconnection. This life is about experience, and divine encounters are often presented as moments of experience. From the divine point of view, it is more thrilling for the journeyer to experience the joy of remembering than to just be told how to reconnect with Spirit. The mastery attained by Jesus shows that he was living a full, rich experience of awakening.

In addition to the many experiences Jesus went through on the road to remembrance, he also received guidance on how the awakening process works. Each connection with these divine beings impressed upon him new elements that he would need to practice in order to realign with his higher spirit-self. These elements make up the seven-step divine model of awakening. These steps are presented in a linear fashion, but Jesus experienced them all at many different times during his journey and on many different levels. The road to spiritual mastery is not straight, but rather a curving, spiraling journey of going deeper into the heart of your being. Like the layers of an onion, you slowly peel back layer upon layer of blocks to reveal your inner spiritual wisdom.

You do not master a step in the divine model in order to move to the next level, because spirituality is about moment-to-moment practice and experience. All moments offer deeper growth and connection with Spirit, so there is no defined starting or ending point within the divine model of awakening. The model represents a cycle of growth where you may begin at any point, knowing that Spirit will guide you through all steps again and again, moving you to a deeper knowledge of self and the divine in our world. In order to follow the divine model, you must learn to use divine guidance and trust your inner wisdom.

Divine Model of Awakening

1. Let go of personal chains binding you to others and this earthly life.
2. Reconnect with your higher spirit-self and your own inner wisdom.
3. Disconnect from conventional wisdom and follow your heart.
4. Connect with the higher source of energy supporting the earthly and divine realms.
5. Discover your higher purpose and create a plan of action.
6. Live as a master in both the earthly and divine realms.

7. Influence others to begin their own journeys home to the divine.

Jesus learned of each step in the divine model as he experienced it. Later, as he moved through the cycle of awakening, he began to see a pattern of practice needed to reconnect with the higher spirit-self. He was given guidance and information he needed in each moment, and he learned to trust in the divine process. In revealing the entire divine model of awakening today, Jesus is giving humanity a great master key to unlocking the secrets of the earthly journey home to Spirit and the integration of the higher spirit-self into daily life. You will experience the power of releasing pain and connecting with Spirit as you move through each of the seven steps of the divine model of awakening, which are presented in subsequent chapters.

To take this journey, you'll need to use your divine senses to practice the divine model of awakening. Divine senses help you to see, hear, know, and feel the divine world around you and connect with your divine guidance. For many of us, our divine intuitive senses have been dormant until now. One of the most exciting parts of the journey is remembering how to use these God-given senses again. Like a child born into this world, you slowly start using these senses, taking baby steps until you master your own set of divine communication skills.

Intuitive senses include the following:

✤ *Clairvoyance,* which is the ability to see images or pictures from divine beings in your mind's inner eye or with your physical eyes. Like a movie or still pictures, you can receive images that communicate what a divine being needs to show you.

✤ *Clairaudience,* which is the ability to hear divine messages through your auditory channels, either as a voice within or as a voice that can be heard right outside of your body. As you clear out old energies blocking this sense, you can discern the distinct voices of the divine.

✤ *Claircognizance,* which is a feeling of knowingness of information being transmitted from the divine, such as an idea that pops into your head. Many people find this sense to be the most comfortable, because it feels like the idea came from within them.

✤ *Clairsentience,* which is a feeling of a divine presence connecting through your emotions or through a feeling expressed physically in your body. People who do hands-on healing may feel a client's pain in their own body, which can be used as a guide to know when the energy has been fully released.

In the beginning of a spiritual journey, divine senses can feel rusty and unused. Like any learned skill, we have to use these senses to feel comfortable and to expand our capability in connecting with the divine. The chakra and energy field visualization in chapter 1 will help you to open up your intuitive senses, as will other meditations in later chapters. Divine senses open naturally as you clear out blocks from your energy system. Part of the process is trusting that these divine senses are real and ready to be used on your spiritual journey.

As a human who experienced the process of opening the intuitive senses, Jesus initially felt confusion and doubt about his newfound divine connection. During his unconscious dreams, it seemed like divine beings spoke with words, but when he consciously connected with them, he heard their words through his inner senses. He had to shift his perception of how he thought the world works and recognize that in linking with the divine, he was going to experience life in an expanded capacity.

As Jesus' dormant divine senses were awakening, they completely changed his awareness of the divine world around him. One day he was walking through a marketplace filled with the smells of live animals, cooking meats, and aromatic spices. He could sense a lightness of energy around the stalls and the many people who busily walked through and bartered for goods. As he approached a woman selling food, he saw that she had a bright white light surrounding her body. She appeared to be cocooned in an egg-shaped energy that moved about her, growing and shrinking as she spoke to patrons in the marketplace.

Jesus stepped back from the line of people outside her stall and watched her interact with customers. When a particularly loud man tried to haggle her below a fair price, the energy around her turned red, grew, and enveloped the man. To Jesus, it seemed like she was trying to crush the man with her energy. The man stepped back, put his hands up in surrender, and paid the woman's asking price.

"She was intimidating him with her power energy," a voice said to Jesus. Now accustomed to hearing the voice of his guardian angel, Jesus knew that she was with him observing the scene.

In his mind, Jesus directed his comments back to his angel. "She seems to be influencing people without even raising her voice."

"Yes, she is basically invading their energy fields with her anger, and they are stepping back and allowing her will to overtake their own. You too will learn how to influence others like this, but not in a way that devalues either of you," the angel said to his inner ears.

"You mean I can use my own body's energy to bend others to my will?" asked Jesus.

"The energy comes from the energy field surrounding your body," said the angel. "See the egg around the woman? Look closely and you can see that she has four eggs around her."

Using his inner vision, Jesus could discern four ovals moving in a circular motion around the woman. One of the eggs moved slowly, while the others spun out of sync at faster rates. Jesus pointed this out to the angel.

"Look at your own field," she said.

Jesus could only discern one huge field around his body. It spun around at a moderate rate. He could see the edges of his egg blur as others walked through his immense field.

"Let's try something," said the angel. "Feel your body being filled with love. See a pink light flow into the crown of your head and let it permeate your entire body and energy field."

She paused as Jesus felt a tremendous energy move into his being. His skin tingled, and he felt very warm.

"Now, as the next person walks by, surround that being with your love," instructed the angel.

A harried-looking man passed in front of Jesus. His brow was furled, and his hands were clenched around a satchel. Jesus willed his egg to envelop the man with love. He could see the field expand and enfold the man, stretching with the man as he hurried past. At about six feet past Jesus, he slowed his pace and turned around, a look of bewilderment on his face. He saw Jesus and retraced his steps back to him.

"Do I know you, sir?" the man asked Jesus.

"No, friend," said Jesus, "we only know each other through our creator."

Unsure, the man looked closely at Jesus and then smiled. Laughing, he clapped Jesus upon the back before turning and continuing upon his way.

"We are all brothers and sisters in the sight of God, dear Jesus," said the angel. "And you shall learn how to help people remember that truth."

Living the Divine Model of Awakening

The key elements of Jesus' divine model of awakening are universal: open up your perceptions to the divine realm by releasing old energy blocking your inherent divinity. Jesus experienced divine encounters pertinent to his divine role as Messiah, as well as divine lessons that helped him to explore and release old issues in his life. Jesus has been called a master of love. He used love as a tool for disarming the angry, calming the fearful, and soothing the wounded hearts of people two thousand years ago. That high form of love came from directly experiencing the healing grace of God in his own life. To feel the grace of God, we have to be willing to let go of things that don't serve us or God well.

Old energy and issues are the stumbling blocks to divinity in our lives. Pain, regret, scarcity, anger, and all other energy that binds us in fear can keep us from feeling God in our life and fully experiencing the divine model of awakening. God's grace holds this world together as well as helps it move smoothly and harmoniously. Grace is given in the Bible when people ask for forgiveness of their sins. The words "sin" and "evil" are often used to describe fear-based actions in the Bible and in our world. These labels are not a part of the divine model of awakening. This model uses the power of love to release pain in our lives and allow us to become who we truly are. In our own hearts, we hold the capability to let Christ's love flow forth from our being. When we desire peace and love in our life, we are most open at that moment to let God's love flow through us, changing our life and touching the world.

Hear now in Jesus' own words his prescription for living within the divine model of awakening:

Dear friends, I ask you now to hear my words and to know that my idea of healing and making people whole through love, forgiveness, and acceptance has not changed. But the human race has changed over the course of two millennia, and language that appealed to people thousands of years ago may not seem relevant to you today. Evil was used then to describe fear-based energy that clouds your awareness of the divine. Evil does not refer to a devil, for only God exists in this universe. There is no fight between good and evil, only the inner struggle of humans facing their own fears. These human-made illusions put on a good show, so much so that the puppet of a devil-god seems real to many. It does not exist, dear ones.

Know that you have the power to release these painful energies that lead you to commit sins. Sins are not trespasses against God but against the self. My original usage of the word "sin" was to describe an act of depravity against the self, perpetrated by the self. The modern-day translation: you hold negative thoughts and fears, and you allow these fears to get the best of you by clouding your true vision of your divine self. Sin means forgetting who you are, which can lead to fear, which can lead to cowardice or hurtful behavior. Sin means living without truth. When you act in sin, you act without regard for the truth of a situation or for others involved.

God does not hold sin against you. He understands that you know not what you've done. The blinders of separation allow for sin to occur, which is a way for all of us to learn more about ourselves. In the divine realm, sin or the potential for it does not exist. The veiled earthly realm allows us to explore what happens when you cut the umbilical cord temporarily with the divine connection to your higher spirit-self. Sin happens, then sin is released.

Releasing sin means letting go energetically of the illusions of pain, fear, and suffering in your life. It feels very real to you in this moment, but when you return to the divine, you take a moment to reassess what you have experienced and most likely, you try again. Why try again and return to Earth as a human? Our very being is about experiencing the all, the sum total of who we are. There is no question that our growth and evolution will continue in this manner.

So how can the divine model of awakening help you in the daily world you exist in now? This, my friends, is the secret to the functioning of the universe. Follow these steps, and you will unravel the mysteries of life in this world as well as the divine. Have courage and strength to let these words move you to action. Does a small part of you remember a world of light within you? Do you feel an inkling of awareness in your being as you read my words? The journey home, fully conscious and awake, begins now.

More than two thousand years ago, I came to reveal the secrets of the divine and allow you to find your way home on your own. The thrill of discovery is immense, and it was my gift to you to share the keys to unlocking the secret doors to the divine. But today, I return to you to give you a modern-day key card to swipe through the doors of eternity, granting you open access to the divine. Brave journeyers, courageous seekers, prepare for departure and join me on this journey. At no other time in the history of Earth have I been more accessible to each and every one of you. My door is open to all, and each may share their journey with me. I will hold your hand, I will lead you, I will walk beside you, and I will bless you with the knowledge of your own eternal life on the other side.

Knowing the Truth of Your Path

A master can only become a master by doing. Jesus awoke and showed great courage by doing, by trying, by challenging himself to be more than just a human having an earthly experience. With the help of Spirit, he began the process of achieving greater connection with his essence and pulling from the greatness of his being to become the Messiah. We too have access to Spirit to help us awaken. The abundance of God is not limited to Jesus, and each of us will encounter wonderful divine beings who will come to us just when we need them during our spiritual journey. Jesus found that his guardian angel was available to assist him during all hours of the day, as well as countless other divine beings who came to him at certain points to lead him through the divine model of awakening.

The divine model of awakening is a universal method that applies to all seekers of divine wisdom. No matter what your divine function is, this divine model can be used to release old pain that blinds you to the divine world around you. You may wonder why Jesus would share this information now. There is a call going around the world to all people to awake and know who they truly are.

Listen now to Jesus, hear his words, and let them touch your heart:

Awake and know that I am not alone in calling you back to the divine world. This earthly world has been a wonderful holiday for many, a time of blissful transport to a world where you may freely explore yourself through limitation and pain. A time where you could discover what you are made of when you feel alone and out of the sight of God. But there comes a time when you must return home from holiday and share the treasures you have found. A call to return home has been issued. You feel it within you, knowing that you can and will release the veils that blind you to your place of origin. Welcome home, dear traveler, the light is burning within you, guiding you home.

3

Step One:
Letting Go of Personal Chains

A s HE progressed along the path to the divine, Jesus found that he needed to release fear-based thoughts he had accumulated during his life. As he worked with his guardian angel and other divine masters, fears would arise and block his budding divine senses and his ability to see, hear, know, and feel the divine world around him, just as they do ours. Through meditation and divine intervention, he learned how to let this fear go from his human energetic system to become an open vessel for God's work upon Earth.

As we move through life, we accumulate many experiences in our human energetic system, which is comprised of the chakras and the physical, emotional, mental, and spiritual energy fields surrounding the body (see page 24). These accumulated experiences are stored energetically in this system as well as in the human body. For example, anger over mistreatment might be stored in your emotional field as well as in the shoulders of your human body. When the issue of mistreatment comes up in another situation, you may feel pain in your back, like you are carrying the weight of the world upon your shoulders. Realizing that you are an inner-connected being, meaning your body is connected with your mind as well as with your energy system, gives you a tremendously valuable key for breaking free from old issues that have inhibited your growth and access to your inner wisdom.

Viewing yourself as an inner-connected energy system of body-mind-energy fields gives you great freedom in controlling your body and your experiences in the world. You, as an energetic being, can choose how you will react to situations and experiences in your life.

You have two choices: you can choose to pull from old energy in your energetic system to form your response, or you can choose to access new energy from your inner wisdom, which extends beyond the energy system of the body.

The automatic choice is to react using what you know, meaning that you can pull from the old energy stored in your energetic system and respond with a familiar pattern of behavior. In the example of anger over mistreatment, you may pull from the emotional field and feel a burden upon your shoulders. You may feel that everyone is out to get you, and that you always have to be on your guard so that no one can take advantage of you. In this defensive state, you may misread the situation and perceive that you need to harden your shell to keep others from hurting you. These old patterns can keep us from leading a life filled with peace, love, and compassion, and yet we often continue to use these behaviors until we become aware that we need to try something new.

The second choice is to pull from a power greater than yourself in this moment: your divine connection to inner wisdom. When you access your inner wisdom, you are opening up energetically to the power of God to work wonders in your life. You tap into a knowledge that expands beyond the tiny energetic system of your human body, forever opening your inner link with Spirit. You use your inner-connected system by integrating and aligning the intentions you hold within your body, mind, and energy fields to access your divine databank of wisdom. You, as an energetic being, become a beacon, a light source for the divine wisdom of God to flow through. You allow the light of Spirit to illuminate your life and old energy patterns, giving you new options for responding and interacting with others. As you move through each step of the divine model of awakening, you will learn techniques for easily accessing your inner wisdom to assist you in all aspects of your daily life.

To pull from this new energy, you have to begin the process of clearing out the old energy stuck in your energy fields. Old energy gums up your divine pipeline, blocking divine insights from reaching your conscious mind. Old pain and patterns of behavior, feelings of separation, and fears of not being connected to God block the pipeline, keeping you from feeling God's presence in your life. When you release this fearful energy, the block is removed and your ever-present inner connection with the heart of God is revealed. Clear chakras and energy fields allow for clear guidance to flow through into your being and change your life.

As you begin your journey to freedom from the chains of limited interactions and perceptions, divine help with this energetic release process will come in many ways. Meditation, chakra-clearing visualization, and other tools that use the power of your intention offer the divine an opening to provide you guidance and assistance. When you do the work of clearing out old energy, you are never alone in the process. You are consciously realigning your will with the will of God and allowing the essence of your higher spirit-self to be expressed through your human body. This was the powerful key Jesus used to become the Messiah.

Jesus again experienced this divine help in further clearing out his energetic system while meditating in a field. The cool evening air gently tousled his hair, and he felt good. In his meditation, he could see colors swirling about him. Sometimes the whirling energy would take form, such as that of a person's face or a beautiful grove of trees. Then the energy would dissolve and reform into another shape.

The colorful energy turned purple and jumped about before Jesus, taking form as a very tall man. He appeared to be ten feet tall, wearing flowing robes and carrying a staff. He seemed to solidify before Jesus' eyes until Jesus felt as though he could reach out and touch him.

Suddenly Jesus sensed that this presence had shifted into human form. Somewhat alarmed, he stopped meditating and quickly opened his eyes. Standing there before him was the man from his meditation. The man exuded a glowing golden energy, and Jesus was bathed in his light.

Rising to kneel before this being, Jesus whispered, "Father, you have blessed me with your presence."

"Let your light shine as brightly as mine, my dear Jesus," God said as he bent and placed his hand upon the chest of Jesus.

A tremendous power surged through him, and Jesus felt emotions wrenching from his body. He saw scenes passing before his eyes: yelling at his brother, taunting a childhood friend, stewing at his father over a disagreement, fearing for the safety of his mother, and grieving over the death of a beloved relative. All of these images flowed like water out of his being. After the final memory slid from his consciousness, Jesus looked up at God.

"There are many memories, many reasons for the pain that you have held close in your being," said God, as he moved his hand to rest upon Jesus' head. "Let them out now. This is but one layer of pain in your being. Now that you know that you no longer need it, you may let it go on your own."

The loving light of God slowly faded, and Jesus was alone in the field. He felt incredibly light and energized. And yet he knew that he had more work to do to become the true Messiah of the people.

Prison Cells of Self, Family, and Society

Just like Jesus, we can learn how to release the energetic burdens of fear-based thoughts, feelings, and emotions on three levels: self, family, and society. Ranging from the personal level to the impersonal level, our identity can be rooted in our perception of the self, our relationship within the family system, and our place in the structure of society and our ability to follow societal norms. Fears stored within the energetic system can ricochet back and forth from the personal level to the impersonal level, perpetuating the fear. We can become trapped in a fearful state, repeatedly analyzing the situation and building up a big energetic case to support the original fear-based feeling. Energetic release on all levels is needed to open a clear connection with your inner wisdom and stop the old patterns of pain.

The physical shell of the human body acts like a closet for the energy of your being. The four energy fields that hang around your body act as energy magnets for experiences, emotions, thoughts, and divine connections. These fields hold all energy from any earthly life you have experienced, and you pull from this closet to react to the world around you. Personal transformation is about cleaning out your closet so that you can return to the divine realm with a clean slate and move to another level of awareness. A clean closet means holding no ill will toward others from experiences or harboring any illusions of pain, fear, anger, disease, or worries about scarcity in your being.

During his lifetime, Jesus worked to let these illusions go, but he found that the constant challenge of daily life required him to develop moment-to-moment practices for keeping his mind and heart clear of these fears. Just as we need to periodically clean out old clothes from our physical closet, we also need to have a spiritual practice that opens and guides us to new wisdom. Spiritual mastery is demonstrated when you know that you can let pain and fears go no matter how often they arise. In a way, the first time you decide to release old energy is the moment when you begin to access and live your inner mastery. As you continue along the path, you will gain greater insight and strength in moving as a master through your world. Spiritual mastery is the recognition that every moment is a continual opportunity to go deeper into the heart of God. Jesus demonstrated this during his entire journey on Earth. He shared the wisdom he gained through his deep inner connection, but he always reminded his followers that they too could reach inner mastery on many different levels. Masters are always growing and changing, touched by every experience that allows them to know themselves on a deeper level.

Each moment of our life offers the opportunity to remember our eternal connection with God and let go of old fears. In the Western world, this remembrance has been difficult because we so concern ourselves with materialistic desires not based on the spiritual laws of abundance and mutually beneficial attainment of goals. These spiritual laws are based on the energetic principle that when you tap into the abundance of Spirit, you pull from a greater power to actualize success on many levels in your life. But we often don't pull from that divine power to make our dreams come true. Instead, our fears and anxiety about becoming successful stand in direct opposition to the abundance Spirit could provide if we chose to work with the power of God. To open a flowing connection with the abundance of Spirit, we have to let go of these old fears of self, family, and society.

We may fear that if we unlock our closets and let go of old

patterns of behavior, we will not be able to function in an overly competitive world. We fear life within the closet and life outside the closet, but ultimately both reside within one fearful prison cell of separation from the Spirit of God.

In the moment before change occurs in our life, we often look deeply at our motivations for trying something new and question why we really need to make a change. We may ask ourselves, "What is my divine purpose? Why am I here on Earth?" These questions of existence touch us on many different levels, including physically, emotionally, mentally, and spiritually. Oftentimes the fact that we don't know the answer leads us to something new as a way to understand our existence on Earth. In taking this journey of the heart, the answer to these questions will be revealed over time.

For me, the journey to understanding the nature of my existence has started with letting go of old preconceived notions about my life. "What is the meaning of life? Why am I here on Earth?" I have asked Jesus during my own journey. The pain of releasing old energy from the abuse of my childhood has freed many parts of my spirit, and yet it also has opened up other painful areas that I need to understand. As I continue to let go of fears that shield me from the divine, I have come face to face with the undeniable existence of the divine realm. But my mind still races and tries to conceal the divine from me, wanting to return to a prior state of ignorance where I am not challenged by the stark contrast of the pain of my life and the undeniable love of God. As I feel the love of Spirit, I also feel the pain of how I have lived and viewed myself. My old preconceived notions of self and the new reality of my existence as a whole, complete being of Spirit create conflict and intensify the need to release old fears of self, family, and society that do not resonate with the love God holds for me. I cannot live as a limited, fearful person when I accept God's strength. God's power will always be greater than my self-imposed limitations.

"The pain of growth and release is an illusion in itself," Jesus said one day in answer to my questions about existence. "You feel deep within your heart your connection to the divine world. You know the truth of who you are. You have experienced countless moments of grace and peace in letting go of old energies that are not a part of your essence. These energies of judgment, pain, fear, and resentment are not the true defining parts of your being, and yet you have allowed them to consume your existence. You ask for the meaning of life, and all you see is fear within you. You ask why you are on Earth, and all you see is limitation of your being. When you ask the questions, you are ready to know the answers. The answers lie within, deep below the outer layers of illusions you have gathered during your travels on Earth. Like an archaeologist, you will dust off these old artifacts and let them see the light of day. But rather than placing them upon your chest as a display of who you are, release them to the light of day. The museum is within you, below the telltale signs of your abuse and pain in this world. The true glory of why you are here is within you, waiting for you to unlock the door and reclaim your divinity."

Releasing Burdens of the Self

We often limit ourselves through our own set of self-imposed burdens and fears. The ego, which acts like a manager of the conscious mind, regulates the reality of our world, determining what is real and what is not. Oftentimes spirituality is not real in the world of the ego. If you believe on some level that you are separate from God, the ego will regulate the flow of information into your conscious mind, only allowing in ideas that reinforce your current belief structure. The ego has served us well in terms of teaching us how to survive in the world, but it can become a part of the illusion of separation between heaven and Earth.

The ego can become attached to many kinds of behavior that separate us from our divinity. We may judge or feel inferior to others, we may feel hatred for those who are different, we may behave like a victim or victimize others, we may lie to or cheat others, or we may deny the existence of God. The voice of the ego can stream forth, creating more fear in our life. You know the feeling when you obsess about something, playing the situation over and over again in your mind, each time finding some new painful element that brings shame into your heart. This function of the ego is not needed when you reconnect with your higher spirit-self. When you consciously decide to reconnect with the divine and realign your conscious mind with your higher spirit-self, you must begin the process of releasing the stronghold of the ego on your world.

Why do we have an ego if it keeps us from knowing the heart of God within?

Listen now as God explains the function of the ego:

There is a divine plan for everything in the universe, including the human mind and its protector: the ego. The ego was designed to hold you in place, to provide an inner foe to conquer. The inner voice of the ego provides energy to create external scarcity, fear, and pain in the world. You all create your worlds using the ego as the sleeping master of pain. What a great challenge the ego has provided humans, a great riddle to solve. It acts as a gatekeeper to finding out the answer to the meaning of life. Get past this sphinx, and you will come to know the glories of living heaven upon Earth. The ego is not eternal, but rather a transient friend who has overstayed his welcome. You may release the ego and reclaim the inner wisdom of your higher spirit-self.

All humans are born with an ego function, and Jesus had developed his own strong ego voice during his youth. Jesus was a strong man with a powerful personality, living in a patriarchal society. As the eldest brother, he enjoyed a certain level of respect from his younger siblings and the men in the community. He was a man of integrity and honesty, but he also had a strong ego voice that kept him sheltered from the voice of the divine world and the hand of God until his time came to awaken as the Messiah.

Before his awakening, Jesus' ego voice would whisper a stream of reality facts to support his life as a man in ancient Israel. His ego would tell him that he was superior to his brother, James, because he had a finer skill in carpentry work and a stronger work ethic. He felt above other men in the community who would drink too much wine and let their work lapse. He felt that it was important to abstain from sexual relations before marriage, so he saw himself as purer than other men who did not. Jesus' ego voice was filled with judgment of others, which separated him from others, and ultimately from the inner heart of Spirit, during his younger years.

Letting go of the ego is a key part of the journey to reconnecting with your divine inner wisdom. If you start on the path to realigning with the wisdom of your higher spirit-self without doing any work to release the ego regulator of consciousness, you will flip back and forth between the duality of living in the fear of the ego and trying to accept the love of God in your heart. Fear and love cannot coexist in your mind, so you will feel a great battle of doubt as the ego tries to maintain order within your thoughts and feelings. Doubt about the validity of your belief in the unseen, the often intangible world of God, will always be at the back of your mind. You will struggle in letting go of old fears in your life, because you will have difficulty believing that the new wisdom of the higher spirit-self is valid in the face of all you have known.

To believe in the new, let go of the old. The key to accessing your inner wisdom lies in your strength to trust that there is more to life than you know in this moment.

Jesus found this key one day while sitting by a hearth with his mother. He had been a bit puzzled by some of his divine encounters and was deep in thought when Mary touched his arm. Startled, he gave her an apologetic smile.

"You seem far away, dear Jesus. What's troubling you?" asked Mary.

Jesus loved his mother greatly and feared her reaction if he told her about his divine experiences.

Before he could speak, Mary said, "I was once visited by an angel, and I believe that I looked very much like you do after it happened."

Jesus jerked his body to face his mother. "Angel? You were visited by an angel?"

Mary nodded.

"Why didn't you tell me? When did it happen?" asked Jesus.

"It happened a long time ago, before your father and I were married. An angel of God appeared to me and told me that I would bring the son of God into the world and that his name would be Jesus," said Mary, tears rolling down her cheeks.

Jesus fell to his knees and held his mother's hands in his own. "Then it is true."

Mary only nodded, touching his cheek.

Alone in bed later that night, Jesus realized how small and petty he had been during his life. He vowed that he would no longer judge others, for he did not hold that right. He began meditating, using a technique given to him by his angel, to release the thoughts that chained him to a limited existence.

The following meditation connects you with Saint Germaine, who holds divine healing powers of redemption and release. Jesus received assistance from many masters to do ego-release work, but Saint Germaine was chosen for this meditation because of his devotion to helping all who wish to open their conscious minds to the greater wisdom of Spirit.

Meditation for Releasing Burdens of Self

Find a comfortable place to sit. Close your eyes and breathe deeply, filling yourself with white light with each breath.

Feel a warm, colorless energy running through your body, rushing through your arms and legs, and filling up your chest and head. See this energy swirl and move quickly through your body, until the edges of your human form look slightly blurred. See the four energy fields that encircle your body. Move the warm energy quickly around your fields until all four fields have blurred edges.

Call now upon Saint Germaine, asking him to come to your side. Ask this divine being to use his violet flame of redemption to clear out all ego energy that is blocking your awareness of the divine world. Look closely at your body and energy fields and watch as the violet flame encircles old energy and pulls it out of your being.

Feeling lighter and refreshed, see a golden pink light enter through your crown, filling up your body and its four energy fields. The blurred edges are now firm again. See yourself as a being of golden pink light.

Open your eyes knowing that you have released pain that is no longer yours to carry.

Releasing Burdens of Family

We all are aware of our place in our family structure. Some may have been the bad girl or boy, others the brain, some the black sheep, while others were the invisible child. The dynamics of our family shape us as people in this world, and these beliefs can deceive us when we become adults.

We can end up perpetuating our childhood strategies for survival by using them to function in the world as adults. As children dependent upon our parents, we often learned how to manipulate and pull them in different directions to get what we needed. We may have learned the power of negative reinforcement, because we had to act out to get our needs met. Or we may have negated our own needs in service to others because we could not expect to get our needs met. We were shaped by a cycle of behavior, and we may perpetuate the same attitudes and beliefs as adults in raising our own children, whether they work or not.

Reliance upon others in the family structure can shield us from our own inner greatness, leading to a struggle for limited resources within the family system. Scarcity in childhood can drive us to fear that our needs will not be met physically, emotionally, intellectually, and spiritually. Competition for limited resources can develop, creating the need for allies and competitors in the family. We can jostle our brothers and sisters, vying for attention, love, and food. Along the way, we develop strategies for survival in a limited environment. As children, we assume that the world functions the way our family environment does. As adults, we bring these patterns out into the workforce and the community, setting up even more competition for resources. We may see someone behaving in a way that sets off our own inner vigilance, our gatekeeper of resources, and we will lash out using familial behaviors that have worked for us in the past, whether or not they're appropriate in the present.

Despite the fact that we all grow up in an environment of scarcity, every life lived on Earth is a noble life. You will learn how to let your core essence of love, peace, harmony, faith, and hope shine forth. Can peace triumph over pain? Can a small part of you step out of the shadow of anger to help another person? Can you release the bonds of this limited life and reclaim the greatness of your higher spirit-self? Jesus himself took this journey to feel the glory of reconnecting with the divine within. But he had to overcome the burdens of being raised in a family trying to survive in the world of scarcity that was ancient Israel. He had to find the strength to let go of fears created by the dynamics of existing within a family structure.

Jesus had been helping his father, Joseph, in the barn one day, when his brother James came in. James had always envied his older brother, and as he entered his teen years, he wanted to prove himself as Jesus' equal.

James looked on in interest as Jesus was hammering together a wooden frame for his father. Jesus could see the envy in James's demeanor, for he knew the competition his brother felt with him. As he finished the piece, he looked up to see his guardian angel appear behind James. She placed her hands upon James's shoulders, and Jesus immediately sensed a change in his brother's attitude.

"Nice work," James said with a smile, as he turned and walked out of the barn.

"What miracle did you just perform?" Jesus asked his angel.

"I asked your brother's higher spirit-self if I could release the energy of judgment he was feeling toward you. That energy is not a part of his true being, so the glory of his divinity shone through when the clouds of pain were lifted."

Jesus soon learned how to release his own childhood feelings of pain, fear, resentment, and anger. In releasing these burdens, he could reclaim positive family experiences that strengthened his resolve to live a Spirit-driven life. Those empowering experiences gave him courage to live a new life in the light of God and to reach deeper within his being for his divine wisdom.

Hear now as Jesus explains how family burdens play into your ability to reconnect with your higher spirit-self:

My dear friends, your fears fall into ranges, from those affecting the personal self to perceived threats from impersonal society. Family fears fall right in the middle, where your identity has become entangled with the lessons of surviving in your family and with your fears of how you are perceived by the greater society. Life in a family affects our development, including our personality traits of love, compassion, strength of character, and humility. We learn many styles for expressing these personality traits, some that enhance our growth and others that inhibit our mastery of life.

Releasing burdens of family means that you are willing to see life in a new way based upon new experiences of connecting with your inner wisdom. As you clear out old fear-based energy, you will immediately receive new insights to replace old thoughts and behaviors. It is your conscious choice to incorporate these new learnings into your life and to live in greater connection with Spirit. Letting go of your automatic response to old familial behaviors does not mean that you are dishonoring your family or that you do not love your family. It means that you recognize that because of past circumstances that limited your life within your family, you are choosing to find new ways of living your life now. We do not honor the past by living in the past, continually creating situations that mirror our childhood experiences. We honor our family by embracing experiences that provided us with love, compassion, strength of character, and humility, and using them to grow even more in these areas. Honor those things of value that you received, and let go of those things that did not serve you.

Jesus offers the following meditation for divine seekers to let go of familial burdens. Just as Jesus continued to consciously release the many layers of old energy clouding his being, use this meditation often when you feel past burdens limiting your present life.

Meditation for Releasing Burdens of Family

To begin, find a comfortable, quiet place to sit. Relax your body, allowing your shoulders to release the tensions of the day. Breathe deeply, down into your lower abdomen. Visualize a white light flowing into the crown of your head, filling your body from your toes up to the top of your head. Allow the light to completely relax your body. With your eyes closed, see Jesus enter the room and sit down behind you.

He places his hands upon your shoulders and softly says to you, "Walk with me, along this path of love. You are a beloved child of light, a being of tremendous greatness. I hold you close, dear to my heart. Know that God dwells within. All you need to do is remember his presence and peace within your life."

Feel the love of Jesus filling your being. See his purple light surround and protect you. Know that peace is yours and the pain that you carry within is not your own.

Jesus stands and moves in front of you. He holds out his hands, letting you know that the burdens you carry are not your own. Name these burdens now out loud, *Pain, fear, anger, disease, judgment, scarcity, brutality, indifference, poverty.*

Say out loud with Jesus, *These energies are not my own. I release these energies. I no longer carry these burdens. I release these energies to Jesus to return to the divine source of love. Transform me now and for all time.*

Watch now as these burdens are pulled from your being into the hands of Jesus. Feel the energy slide out of your being, knowing that you bid it farewell and need not retrieve it for review. As the last bit of energy leaves you, Jesus smiles as he releases white doves from his hands. Feel your own heart lighten and soar through the heavens.

Jesus now places his golden hands of love upon your head and heart. Golden white energy streams into your being, renewing and refreshing you.

Open your eyes knowing that you are loved.

Releasing Burdens of Society

Just as self-imposed and familial burdens weigh us down, society's burdens drag down our hearts. Our world is often not a pretty place, filled with crimes against humanity, nature, and our inner divinity. In our state of separation, we can act without thought, believing that our actions do not affect others or hurt people in the community around us.

We all are a part of a local and global community. We know our neighbors, keep up on the interactions between government leaders, and read about events on the other side of the world. We are interconnected by the news media and the Internet, so that no event, big or small, goes unnoticed. We are taught history in school so that we know what our ancestors created before us. We determine cause and effect from their actions, and we inherit their legacy of laws, rules, social norms, and regulations.

The actions of past and present individuals in our society become our burdens to carry. The legacy of wars, those century-old conflicts among countries, shape how we interact locally and globally in the world. If we are Muslim, we are born into a predetermined set of expectations to which we must adhere. Catholics learn rules that must be abided by, and Jews must follow regimens in order to adhere to their religious doctrine. Californians inherit certain expectations of freedom in their state, while a Parisian knows how to behave during a five-course meal.

In addition to set expectations for how certain groups of people should behave with others, we inherit old rivalries for money, power, and strength among groups in geographic areas around the world. You may be uptown, downtown, or on the wrong side of town, and the treatment you receive is based on your status. Status also is expressed within the microcosmic society of businesses, where competition for respect develops between management and labor, often leading to power struggles and alienation among employees.

All of these elements make up societal burdens. "What would the Joneses think if I went outside in a pink bathrobe to pick up my newspaper?" We may speculate on many different levels before undertaking any task. We look outside our windows, questioning how our actions will be perceived in our community of friends, among business colleagues, and with strangers we may meet on the street. Our community becomes our mirror as well as our prison, keeping us in line on the straight and narrow, very much entrenched in being like everyone else.

When society's expectations are based on judgment and fear, they shield us from the divine world. We flog ourselves when we perceive even the tiniest bit of judgment from others. We do things at night so that others won't see, when we know that our actions will not be accepted. We place society's accepted norms and conventions in our hearts, and we can pull from that judgmental energy when we feel fear over our chosen actions or behavior. We perpetuate these societal norms ourselves, through the power of our energetic system. Every time we buy into a convention of society, we contribute energy to the continuation of that socially accepted behavior. Some societal norms, such as the practice of spanking children or unequal treatment of different social classes, don't serve us well. Yet some may continue these behaviors because they are accepted on some level within society.

We carry the pain of societal burdens and our own interpretations of them. Perceived judgment from the world at large can keep us in a box, unwilling to try something new for fear of being labeled unacceptable or different. Releasing the burdens of society means letting go of the outer critic from your inner heart. Reaching inside to a higher wisdom requires the belief that there is more to the world than what society has shown us, and that new forms of living in communion with Spirit are acceptable.

Jesus knew the societal burdens of his day: the strife between Romans and Jews, insistence on a strong work ethic, and a limited notion of acceptable ways to worship God. He knew that people could be volatile over religious issues and that his new teachings would spark controversy. Yet he also knew that God would give him courage to release these societal burdens, freeing him to do his work.

One afternoon, his guardian angel appeared to Jesus while he was sitting around a table with some friends. Knowing that the others could not see the angel, Jesus was about to stand up to leave the room, but the angel motioned for him to remain seated.

"You all form an energy portal around the table," said the angel to the inner ears of Jesus. "All of your energy fields are meeting in the center of the table, creating a powerful vacuum for pulling out old pain from your being."

Using his inner eyes, Jesus looked around the table at his friends and saw that their energy fields converged in a funnel of energy opening up to the heavens.

"As the Messiah, you will release your own pain as well as the pain of others. In this moment, you can release another layer of energy from your being as well as a layer from your friends. Repeat out loud what I say to you," instructed the angel.

Jesus immediately felt fear. "What would you have me say to these men?"

"They are not conscious of the divine world, and you need their consent to do the release," replied the angel. "I will guide you through the process."

Jesus took a deep breath and began to follow the guidance of the angel. He slammed his hand upon the table. Startled, the men turned toward him.

"I can no longer live with the pain of the fear we live under in Israel. It is eating up my very heart. Do you not agree with me?" he asked his friends.

The men looked at Jesus with concern and agreed that they too were saddened and angered by the state of affairs in Israel, and its impact upon their own lives.

"Here and now, I pledge that I will no longer let this pain eat me alive. Take my hands, brothers, and together we will rise above a crime that is not our own," said Jesus, as the men joined hands around the table.

"And now," the angel told Jesus, "ask the men to have a moment of peace with you."

As the men held hands in silence, Jesus could feel an energy pulling pain from his body. It felt magnified, different from his first release with God, and he gently swayed back and forth. In his mind's eye, he could see the vortex to the heavens pulling out dark energy from all of the men's fields.

As the release ended, Jesus spoke. "Brothers, we have shared a communion of the heart and mind, a moment of peace in a world filled with injustice. Despite the pain around us, together we have risen above to a silent place within. I feel that I know the divine within you all, and it has changed me greatly."

The men looked upon Jesus with wonder, feeling his hope and strength fill them anew. The angel gazed upon him, smiling.

Just like Jesus, you also have the ability to release old societal blocks using the same energy techniques in group situations. When a group of people comes together, their energy fields can combine in a powerful vortex for release. Jesus gained consent for a group release by identifying the societal issue that he felt weighed most heavily upon them all. He then asked for a moment of peace, which aligned the will of the men with the will of Spirit for a life without the burden of societal pain. He used his inner connection and strong intentions to direct Spirit in letting these fears go for all present. You also can release societal fears with others or on your own using the following meditation.

Meditation for Releasing Burdens of Society

Stand by a wall and place one arm upon the wall for support (for groups, stand in a circle and hold hands). Closing your eyes, breathe deeply, filling your body with white light.

Say out loud any societal burdens that weigh upon you, such as, *financial status, home size, material possessions, job title, race, religion, gender, spiritual beliefs.*

After stating all burdens, say, *I willingly release these societal burdens. They are not my own.*

Visualize all four energy fields around your body spinning together in a counterclockwise motion. See the old energy flowing out of your fields and up to the heavens. When your release feels complete, stop the spinning of the fields. Now spin all fields in a clockwise motion, repeating, *I willingly release these societal burdens. They are not my own.* Again, stop the spinning when the release is finished.

Look at your fields, knowing that you have released a layer of burdens. Now welcome the loving light of Jesus to fill your being. See a purple light flow into the crown of your head, filling your body and energy fields.

Open your eyes feeling full of divine love and acceptance.

Now-Moments of Release

After a big cleaning of your closets, there may be a temptation to throw some things back into this clear space. Sometimes when we're tired, we say, "Oh, I'll take care of that later." Later comes, and it may have to wait even longer. It's important to develop the habit of using now-moments of releasing, which means releasing any blocking energy the moment that it occurs. You may not have time to stop and meditate, but you can mentally say, *I willingly release this energy. I choose not to hold it as my own*. This statement of intention clears the road ahead and allows you to continue unfettered on your journey.

Jesus grew into his role as the Messiah by creating a "now-practice," which incorporates now-moments of releasing, meditation, time spent in nature renewing the soul, and time spent with others to grow friendships as well as opportunities to let go of old triggering energy. A spiritual path for most people will not be spent hidden in a cave or in a monastery. We all have active lives filled with commitments to family and friends. The key to living life as a spiritual master like Jesus is to view your spiritual practice as simple. It is simple to decide to let pain go and to diligently do now-moments of releasing. It is simple to schedule at least ten minutes a day for quiet meditation time and to take a moment to feel the cool wind of nature upon your cheeks. It is simple to hold the intention in your heart that you are ready and able to accept new wisdom and a new way of living life. Your attention and energy follow your intention, so let your intention be strong and simple: *I willingly let go of pain in my life on all levels with the loving help of Spirit to guide and renew me.*

As Jesus developed his now-practice, he found that he needed to be vigilant in clearing his energy. Old judgmental thoughts would arise, creating a wedge between him and another person. He would quickly let the energy go with a statement of intention. Other times he would call upon his guardian angel when the energy would stubbornly stick within his being, chattering away reasons why it had to stay within him.

One afternoon after an argument with his brother James, Jesus sank down under a tree and placed his head in his hands.

"Why does it have to be so hard, Lord?" he asked.

Immediately his angel appeared beside him.

"Stand up now," commanded the angel.

Jesus looked at her in disbelief, but he stood.

"Run in place," she instructed.

Jesus jogged under the tree. Five minutes passed, and he looked at her inquiringly. Still pumping his legs, he asked, "Why do you have me run, angel?"

"Why do you choose to continue to run?" countered the angel.

Jesus stopped. Breathing heavily, he bent forward and placed his hands upon his knees to cool down. A few moments later, he straightened up and smiled at his angel.

Shaking his head, he said, "I fear that I have been given the angel of torture."

After they laughed together, he continued, "I know, dear angel, that you have shown me that I choose my misery. I let go of this pain, but it seems that it never leaves me. I still get angry with my brother as if I have not changed at all."

"In your heart, dear one, you have changed," said the angel, placing her hand upon his shoulder. "Each time you let go of this pain, you get closer to the heart of God within you. The pain that you still hold within you beckons to you, whispering loudly that it hurts too much to do this work. Know that pain is only an illusion. It only exists if you allow it to. Remember the love within you. Look for the love rather than the pain."

The angel then handed Jesus a beautiful red apple. It shone brightly, pure red with a golden light surrounding it.

"Do you see an apple before you or do you see the love of God for you?" asked the angel.

Just like Jesus, we all choose how to view what life gives us. Every situation offers an opportunity to remember our abundant connection with God. We can choose to let God's love guide every action in our life, seeing this love in every living thing that he lovingly created for us.

4

Step Two:
Opening to the Wisdom of
the Higher Spirit-Self

RELEASING old energy is just the first step to reconnecting with your divine higher spirit-self. As you begin to shed old layers of energy, your perception of the divine world increases, and your ability to receive divine guidance directly from your higher spirit-self opens up. Like a freshly cleaned window, you allow the light of God to penetrate your being, forever changing your perception of life on Earth and of the divine world around you.

As you journey into the inner realms of your being, the first person you meet is usually not your higher spirit-self. Most people will connect first with their guardian angel to receive guidance on accessing this new place of wisdom. During meditation and through conscious guidance, your guardian angel will help you to release old ego beliefs that have kept you separate from your higher spirit-self. As you go deeper into Spirit, you will encounter divine masters who also will assist you with this process. As you let go of old fear and limiting ego structures, you are then ready to let the higher spirit-self descend into your conscious awareness and accept a new belief structure based upon the love and abundance of Spirit.

Jesus worked diligently with his guardian angel and divine masters to release old blocks from his life so that he could let his inner wisdom flow into his being and become an open instrument of God. Based on the strength of his intention to reach the inner world of God, he linked directly with his higher spirit-self not long after he began releasing energy. There are no set time frames for directly connecting with the higher spirit-self. Your own unique journey will unfold in its own way based upon the power of your will and your intention to link with your inner Spirit.

Jesus experienced his first connection with his higher spirit-self while walking along a desert road, deep in thought about his energy work. He was thinking about how much progress he had made in changing his attitude toward James when a voice said to his inner ears, "Take it one step deeper, brother."

He stopped walking and tuned in with his inner eyes to see who was speaking to him. He did not perceive any divine beings around him, but he felt a presence. He scanned his own body and saw a huge divine being superimposed over his body. This being felt very familiar to him, so he was not frightened at all.

"I know you as brother, and yet I do not know your name," said Jesus.

"I am you, dear Jesus, you on a higher level of existence," replied his higher spirit-self.

Jesus sat down by the side of the road. He closed his eyes so that he could fully tune in to his higher spirit-self with his inner eyes and ears.

"I feel your strong energy and a tremendous love for you," said Jesus, as a shiver of energy ran down his back.

"And I feel a great love and respect for you, dear Jesus," said his higher spirit-self. "You took this journey knowing that you would have to awaken, blind and deaf, to the real world around you. And yet you have worked to release the pain of this life so that we may reunite as one. You are the master of this world, but there are other masters within our essence. You started the journey home, and you issued the clarion call to other parts of our being to stand together again as one."

Jesus sat in silence, thinking about the vastness of his being. Suddenly, he felt himself expanding outside of his body. He could feel himself losing human form and becoming the energy of the universe, encompassing all within and without the world. He could feel the heart of God pumping in the center of the energy, a unifying force holding all parts together. He felt like God, and yet he felt like himself. He felt like the universe, and yet he felt like the Earth. He felt at the center of all, and yet he felt at the center of one.

Slowly, his awareness retracted until he was again sitting by the side of the road.

"I am within you now, dear Jesus," said his higher spirit-self. "Together, we will unite the mysteries of your being."

Just like Jesus, you will link with your higher spirit-self in a glorious moment of reconnection. When you first meet your higher spirit-self, it may take a moment to recognize this eternal part of your being that exudes pure love, wisdom, faith, and acceptance. You may not have felt or recognized such a pureness of energy within yourself before. This is just the beginning of the process of letting these eternal qualities shine through your being.

Entrapping the Ego

As you begin to release old burdens of self, family, and society, you will find that the ego stronghold in your mind begins to loosen. This is one of the goals of meditation: ease the chatter of the mind so that the true essence of the being may shine through. But there are additional techniques Jesus used to get beyond the power of the ego in order to increase his direct access to the wisdom of his higher spirit-self.

Jesus would meditate daily, usually in late afternoon before his evening meal. He felt most open to guidance at this time, because his ego had been hard at work all day and was more receptive to taking a break from control. At this time, Jesus would visualize entrapping his ego and releasing it to the heavens. His other energy-releasing meditations worked well for releasing specific actions, emotions, thoughts, and burdens related to self, family, and society, but he felt compelled to work specifically on letting go of the ego.

During one of his afternoon meditations, he felt nagging thoughts tugging at his concentration. He recognized the voice of his ego, telling him that he was no good and could never be the son of God.

"Angel, please guide me now," Jesus said, and his guardian angel immediately appeared. He still worked with his angel on letting go of old energy. "This ego voice will not stop, and I'm having a hard time focusing on my meditation."

"Let's entrap the ego and let it know that it is not needed," replied the angel. She then told him how to visualize this process.

Jesus sat quietly and looked within his body and energy fields. He could see dark areas of energy, which were old sites of fear and emotional pain that the ego would pull from. He released this energy by spinning his energy field. He watched as the dark energy flew out of his field and body. Scanning his being again, he could see clear spots where darkness had once reigned.

His ego voice stepped in, saying, "I think you're done. No more for today. You are tired and need to eat now."

Following the guidance of his angel, Jesus visualized white light pouring into his crown, penetrating deep within his being. He started at his feet and saw the white light fill in all areas that once held dark energy. Moving up through the legs, lower torso, upper torso, arms, and head, he methodically filled in all empty spaces within his being with white light.

When he completed this process, he said to his ego, "Ego, I am full and complete. Your work here is done. Thank you for protecting me, but your services are no longer needed. Return to the light to help others with your energy."

He immediately felt a lightening in his body, and a sense of completion filled his being. He was then able to continue meditating.

You too can entrap the ego by filling up your being with white light. After releasing old energy through spinning your energy fields, follow the same process Jesus used and methodically fill up spaces you perceive as empty with white light. Even if you cannot see the actual empty spaces with your inner eyes, visualize filling all spaces in your body with light.

The job of the ego is to keep us busy and full, regardless of the quality of energy we are holding. Old, dark, fear-based energy works well to fill up our bodies, and the ego sees its job as successful when we are occupied with our own thoughts, whether they are positive or negative. You can entrap the ego by clearing out this old energy and filling your body with divine light. Let the ego know that you are full, and it will begin to leave your being willingly.

After practicing entrapping the ego, you will find a remarkable difference in the clarity of your thinking. New thoughts will come to you, and you'll find that you don't think within the box of everyday reality. By letting go of the ego, you allow the voice of the higher spirit-self to be heard. This voice is directly linked with God and the wisdom of the universe.

The Simple Path of Wisdom

Connecting with our higher spirit-self is simple when we understand which road to follow, the language of the road signs, and the culture of the new divine beings we meet. We can find the right road when we realize that the road is the divine plan we have come to Earth to actualize. We hold this divine map of purpose in our memory, and when we decide to take this journey of awakening, we begin to remember how the trip is taken. We can understand the language of the road signs when we open up our intuitive translators to receive divine guidance. And we can feel comfortable traversing this divine territory among the natives when we remember that the world of Spirit is based upon love, peace, and abundance. We cannot use human standards to judge new experiences with Spirit. What you know about life is not what life is really about when you connect with Spirit. Life is greater, fuller, and richer than what meets the eye.

You may look in the mirror and see one person before you, a human being with two eyes, a nose, and a mouth. You may like what you see in the mirror, or you may critique the face staring back at you. You see one face, but below the surface of your human shell exists a divine energy connection that is awaiting full activation.

And this activation is a simple process.

Within your body, you hold seven chakras that, when fully clear and opened to divine light energy, will connect you to your higher spirit-self. Your energy fields—the physical, emotional, mental, and spiritual fields surrounding your human body—dampen and block this divine connection with old veiling energy. When you clear out this old energy, your divine connection sparks to life, and you can reconnect with the wisdom of your higher spirit-self.

It sounds simple because it is. In our state of separation, we have built walls around ourselves, shutting out God and the divine world. We create barriers of confusion and denial. In a state of sleeping power, we put up our shields. In a state of awakened power, we can take down our shields.

Hear now as Jesus explains the powerful simplicity you have discovered:

> Dear ones, we have learned that our fear-based thoughts and emotions are only energy and can be released. But have you yet realized the power of this concept and the magnitude of its impact on your life? You think in concrete terms of weight and physicality based on the earthly realm you live in. Walls, fences, and barriers seem solid, and you feel that you must labor to break them down. Energy, however, is not solid. Rather, it's flowing, rushing, always changing. You work hard to keep this old energy in place, but before long, the effort to maintain stasis outstrips the effort needed to let the energy go. Let it go and reconnect with your higher spirit-self. It's as simple and powerful as that.

See the simplicity of the journey, and you will find the road of wisdom. This road has been traveled by many a spiritual seeker, and lanterns placed by others along the path will guide your way. Many people who we call saints have chosen the same spiritual path of wisdom as Jesus did to guide them through this life, living in an elevated state of awareness.

Saint Francis of Assisi chose to be an instrument of God, asking how he could be used to bring forth the messages of the divine to heal the souls of a world hungry for forgiveness and the glance of God. Francis connected into the Christ energy, which allowed love, forgiveness, and acceptance to flow through his being. He touched many people's hearts with his simple message of surrender to the God energy within. See the simplicity, and the road of wisdom will appear.

Jesus began to see the simplicity of his own journey as his higher spirit-self unwound the layers of bondage in his soul. After his first conscious connection with his higher spirit-self along the road, Jesus realized that he had been playing the game too hard, comparing his divine journey with his earthly life of strife and hard work.

"You cannot equate the divine journey with an earthly existence," his higher spirit-self said to Jesus while he lay awake in bed one night. "You push, you labor, you cry. You say to yourself, 'Look, I'm working very hard here, doing very hard things. It hurts, but I'm strong enough to get through.' That's just a human mentality for a divine function of releasing energy. It's just energy, pure and simple, no matter what labels you attach to it. Say it is hard, and it will be. Say that it is simple to let this go, and it will be. Live the divine now, and the journey will be divine. Pure and simple."

Your higher spirit-self exists in the divine realm with the eternal being, Jesus, and knows him well. Your divine self holds many of the same high-level personality traits as Jesus and so can you, right now in your human form. It's the realization that you can simply hold the powerful intention to become the person you wish that will set you free from the pain and strife of this earthly life. Let go of the burden of struggle, for it does not truly exist when you rely upon the power of Spirit to help you on your journey. Jesus offers the following meditation to help you to simplify your life and learn to see the simple divine truth in all of your experiences on Earth.

Divine Simplicity Meditation

Find a quiet place to sit. Arrange your body in the most comfortable position possible. Relax and breathe deeply, filling your body with white light. Full and complete with this loving energy, sit for a moment and feel your body.

Notice the heavy parts and the light parts in your body. Where in your body would you most like to reside right now? Where do you feel most comfortable and at peace in your body? Go to this place and concentrate upon this peaceful spot. Live within this place of peace. See yourself walking, dancing, running, eating, singing, living in joyful peace in this spot within your being.

Now that you have fully explored this feeling of peace within you right now, expand this feeling into your entire body. Speak to this inner peace, see this inner peace, and direct it to flow throughout your being. It is simple to grow and expand peace, for all growth comes from peace and love.

Simply say, *Peace within my being, flow freely and fill me with your simple glory. Let me know what it is to feel peace within me in every moment.*

Peace is a beautiful color of emerald green. See this color flow forth into your body, filling and renewing every cell, every muscle, every bone, every part of your being. Let peace dwell within you, knowing that peace is yours, that it blesses as well as heals your being.

Now feeling a deep sense of peace throughout your being, state your intentions for your divine journey in terms of its simplicity by saying, *I am peace. I am the peace-giver. I am peace in action. My journey is a blessed event and a joy to participate in. I am one with God. I let go of pain easily and gracefully. I love who I am and who I am becoming. I am a divine being of love and light.*

Sit quietly in this moment of peace and simplicity. When you are ready, open your eyes, knowing that you are simply loved.

Lifting the Veil to the Higher Spirit-Self

The simplicity of the journey is in the eye of the beholder. Ten different people can look at a painting and see ten different things. One may be touched by the image, while another may be dazzled by the color. Each spiritual journey is unique to each individual expression of God. You may be moved physically, emotionally, intellectually, or spiritually, and your inclinations will be expressed during your own awakening.

The level of your need for reassurance during your journey also is unique to your own process of realigning with the higher spirit-self. Your comfort level is affected by how you perceive the miracle of awakening and by your understanding of the simplicity of the energetic release process. Knowing some simple energetic concepts about the divine structure of our universe can help in explaining what is occurring.

A spiritual awakening is just part of the universal birth, death, and renewal process. This awakening is like birth, except this time you are a fully functioning, active participant in the process. Death during a spiritual awakening is the death and release of old ideas and behaviors that haven't served you well during this life. Renewal is the connection of the higher spirit-self with your human vessel, which allows inner wisdom to flow through your consciousness and restore harmony within your being. This process dissolves the veil of separation between heaven and Earth within one human creation of God.

Dissolving the veil between heaven and Earth refers to lifting the cloud of separation between two worlds coexisting in one space. The divine world exists in the here and now, right where you are. Take a moment to consciously experience this veil by separating the vision between your eyes: lay your index finger on your nose, extending it up to the middle of your forehead. On one side of the finger exists heaven, and on the other, Earth. You can see a blur of skin between the two worlds, and yet if you didn't know it was a finger, you might not perceive the barrier as real within your current perception of the world. Remove the finger, and the totality of your world is restored. In like fashion, remove the veil of separation, and the totality of your world will be restored. It has only been a moment of time that has separated you from the divine world and your higher spirit-self.

It may be hard to believe that a mere veil of energy separates us from our awareness of the divine. The scientific exploration of our world has been one way to understand the mysteries of the universe, and scientific reasoning can help us to understand the concept of veils. Find a balloon and blow it up. The rubber shell of the balloon acts like a warehouse for the air molecules forced inside. Tie the balloon, and the air seemingly stays secure within. But over the course of a few days, the air molecules will seep out of the shell of the balloon, and it will collapse. Before that happens, take your full balloon and rub it against your hair. Not only will your hair stand up, but the balloon will stick when placed upon the wall. Charged static electricity keeps the balloon attracted and secured against a surface with opposite polarity, which is the uncharged surface of the wall. You can't see this higher frequency static electricity, but you have proof of a balloon sticking to the wall.

Now apply this scientific reasoning to the theory of the veil of separation. There is an energy shell around the physical universe you exist in now. It vibrates at a high level, so it is not apparent to your physical eyes, which are attuned to perceiving low-level frequencies of physical density. This shell acts like a balloon, holding in the inner world of Earth. Your earthly world seems secure, and yet some, like Jesus, have slipped through the veil and experienced the divine beyond the shell. By following the divine model of awakening, you too create energetic effects by consciously releasing old, blocking energy into the universe. Your results are hearing, seeing, knowing, feeling, and sensing the divine world around you through your intuition. Like static electricity that holds a balloon on the wall, you cannot see with your physical eyes the energetic effects of releasing old energy, but you can perceive it through a greater opening of your intuition. Each time you step through the veil and receive divine guidance through meditation and other intuitive connections, you increase your awareness of the interplay between the earthly and divine realms. As you release old energy and fill your body with divine light energy, you raise the vibration of your being and your ability to perceive a higher-frequency world. Slowly but surely, you dissolve the veil and come face-to-face with your own divine greatness.

Jesus knew that his higher spirit-self had great wisdom and unlimited energy. But he also knew that as the human representative of his higher spirit-self, he needed to dissolve his limited veil of perception between the earthly and divine realms in order to access the wisdom, love, truth, and honor of his essence. It is the decision of the human creation to choose this process. Even though you will receive help abundant in releasing energy, your progress and depth of connection depend upon your will and desire to reconnect with your inner wisdom. After opening the connection with the higher spirit-self, you then must choose to accept and allow this divine part of you to influence your behavior in this world. Your progress upon the path to greater depths of wisdom and the ability to serve yourself and others from a place of mastery hinges upon your acceptance of the gifts offered during your journey. Jesus demonstrated that it is a gift to remember your inner greatness and to use that divine power to serve humanity and achieve peace on Earth.

Jesus chose to accept this gift of mastery many times during his interactions with the ancient people of Israel. One afternoon after working with his father on a project in the barn, Jesus needed a break.

"Father, I'm going to take a walk and refresh myself," he

said, waving to Joseph as he stepped out into the hot sun.

He walked toward the marketplace where he knew some of his friends would be. Many of his compatriots enjoyed taking afternoon tea at a stall run by a lovely young woman. Sure enough, Jesus saw a few of his friends sitting on crates, talking quietly among themselves. But as he approached the stall, a man accosted him. Grabbing Jesus by the arm, he slammed Jesus against the wall. Jesus' friends quickly rose to his side. One of Jesus' friends pushed the man, and he fell onto the dirt floor.

"Stop," Jesus commanded his friend, who was about to kick the man in the face.

Internally, Jesus felt his higher spirit-self enter his being. With his inner eyes, he could see the outline of this being around his physical body.

"Allow me to handle the situation," said his higher spirit-self to his inner ears.

Kneeling down beside the cowering man, Jesus placed a hand upon his shoulder. Extending his other hand, he helped the man to stand up. Keeping his hand upon the man's shoulder, Jesus asked, "Why do you come at me so, friend?"

"I know who you are," the man said, anger screwing up his face. "You are a sympathizer of those who blaspheme the true Roman emperor god."

Hand still upon the man's shoulder, Jesus replied, "It is true, friend, that I believe in only one God, who is the father of us all. But fear not what I believe. Only look to the truth of what you believe. We each walk our own path and shall reach our creator in our own time."

The man turned abruptly, shrugging off Jesus' hand. Pushing his way through Jesus' friends, he disappeared into the crowd in the marketplace.

Jesus sat down with his friends, but did not speak to them. He was noticing a feeling of a thin sheet being lifted from his body. Suddenly his surroundings became brighter, and he could see sparks of energy throughout the marketplace.

"You are in your father's house wherever you go, dear Jesus," said his higher spirit-self.

Just like Jesus, you can pull from a strength that is greater than your own in any given moment. When you access the power and wisdom of the higher spirit-self, you can become who you truly are: a divine being having a human experience. You allow your inner strength and divinity to merge with your human self, creating a more powerful being within and through you. You become a human instrument of Spirit, and the world changes into a more expansive realm of possibilities.

Jesus reconnected with his higher spirit-self and became conscious of the power of every step he made in life. He allowed his higher spirit-self to be expressed through his physical being. For some, this may seem contradictory to what we know about developing as an individual with a strong sense of self. As we mature, we move toward living an independent life, separate from our parents and the ideas of youth. Being our own person is one of the goals of growing up. When we reconnect with our higher spirit-self, we have to grow up again in the spiritual sense. We have to look spiritually at our ideas of independence and realize that to be our own person, we don't have to be separate from God. To truly be a powerful person in this world, we have to accept all parts of our being, including our inherent divinity. At first, the hand of the higher spirit-self may feel bigger than your own, and it may seem like you are dependent upon the wisdom of this being to change your behavior and beliefs. But as you allow your own unique wisdom to be expressed through you, you realize that being an integral part of this exchange makes you a powerful agent of change. Your choice to unify all parts of your being is what makes you a complete person in the eyes of Spirit and an instrument of peace in the world.

Opening the Lines of Communication

As you tap into the wisdom of your higher spirit-self, you realize that you are not a sleeping giant but instead a conscious being of power. And this is the key to the miracle of Jesus' journey to becoming the Messiah. He relied upon his inner strength and his powerful connection with Spirit to live a divine life upon Earth.

Hear now as Jesus shares how to accept this miracle in your own life:

> Dear friends, as you learn more about tapping into your inner greatness, many feelings may arise. Some may feel fear that they are not really connected to a great being of light and love, or that they will never be able to open a strong link with this eternal part of their essence. Others may feel angry, stating that they are in charge of the show and they are not going to let anyone tell them what to do. And some may just

feel joy, happy that they have found the key to a part of themselves they have longed to know. Whatever you are feeling in this moment, know this: God loves you.

You have heard this before, but take a moment and allow me to bring this light of love fully into your being. See yourself as a child. You enter a great room of light. At the other end of the room, you see God sitting in a chair, motioning for you to join him. You run across the room and bound up onto his lap. He embraces you, and you feel a warmth filling you so completely that you don't know where you end and he begins. You look up into his face as he gently touches your cheek. "Welcome home, dear one. I love you," God says, and you know in your heart that you've never really left this place of love.

This is what it feels like to know that you are a part of the great abundant world of God. A part of you is still within the great hall of God, so loved, so complete. This is the part of you that is ready to become a part of your conscious world again. Choose to let this eternal part of your being into your world, and you choose to accept the grace, abundance, and love of God in your life.

Your divine self awaits an invitation into your life. It's as simple as a kiss on the cheek and holding the hand of a beloved.

Listen now as God explains the journey back to your inner soul:

Dear ones, you all have made the choice to come to Earth and explore this world of limitation. Before departing into this great sleep here, you decided upon a plan for your time spent here. Many want to overcome past pains and make amends to others from past lives. Some want to achieve greatness and thrill others in this realm. And some want to help and serve others who are seemingly less fortunate than themselves. You chart your course and jump into an earthly life. Your higher spirit-self does not wave good-bye and wish you good luck, leaving you to your own devices. This being charts your progress and gently nudges you to keep on course. Serendipitous moments are divinely inspired and are used to get you to where you wanted to go. Your higher spirit-self is the divine regulator of your journey and is the keeper of your will and intention for your time spent on Earth. Reconnecting with this being while on Earth is an extremely powerful way to realize the plans you made for this earthly life. This being, who is you on a higher level of consciousness, is the version of yourself that you aspire to be on Earth. Compassionate, loving, and full of joy: this describes your higher spirit-self. Reconnect to the part of you that longs to speak to you again and help you to complete your journey.

Jesus did not have a personal diary that he wrote in, but he did start an active inner dialogue with his higher spirit-self. He would connect with his higher spirit-self daily, moment-by-moment, for guidance and assistance. He felt great joy and relief in having access to this unlimited source of wisdom. Like Jesus, you can access your higher spirit-self through inner dialogue, but you also have the benefit of paper and computers to connect easily with your higher spirit-self through journal writing.

This form of communication is called automatic writing,

which is a technique for releasing the bond of the ego and allowing your higher spirit-self to be heard. It may take practice to become comfortable with this new style of communication, so continue to connect often with your higher spirit-self.

Journaling with the Higher Spirit-Self

Find a quiet space, either in front of a computer or in a comfortable place for writing with pen and paper. Breathe deeply, filling your body with white light. See your fears and worries slip out of your being as you say, *I willingly release any fears to reconnecting with my higher spirit-self.*

Feeling centered and fully within your personal power, ask Jesus to oversee your communication with your higher spirit-self by saying, *Jesus, be with me now as I connect with my higher spirit-self. Please ensure that I am open and loving in my reception of this guidance.*

Write the date you begin your communication. Now write down any questions you have for your higher spirit-self. Sit quietly and allow the answers to come. Write whatever thought expresses itself, allowing your fingers to be guided. Relax and know that your higher spirit-self is responding to your questions.

Now-Moments of Wisdom

You can connect with your higher spirit-self at any time as long as your will and intention are strong. Will and intention drive the world and your place within it. If you feel like your presence is not important and you stand in the background, most likely others will see and treat you the same way. You set forth your intention for yourself and your journey in this world, and it will become actualized in that manner. Your will and intention are just energies that propel you through life. Intentional energy can be moved and shaped at any time. Change the energy propelling you, and you can change your direction. Jesus experienced this change of focus as he connected deeper with his inner essence and began the journey to leading and teaching others.

Jesus received schooling as a boy, but during his late teens he followed in his father's footsteps and worked as a skilled carpenter alongside Joseph. He knew that one day he might change his path, but he felt compelled at that point to assist his father and learn his trade. He felt that in order to honor his father, he should be like his father. While he enjoyed woodworking, he also knew that it would not be his trade for life.

Joseph sensed the conflict in his son. He wanted to help Jesus find his own path, but he had an inner knowingness that Jesus would have to make that choice alone. He knew that great things awaited his son, but he also knew his own responsibility with this sleeping giant: raise him with love and compassion, provide schooling for him, and allow him to find his own path.

Joseph could see the changes Jesus was going through. He felt the shift in Jesus' attitude and saw a personal strength developing like no other he had seen before. Jesus was becoming a powerful man, and yet his strength did not lie in hatred of a group or reigning over others. He did not wish to control but rather to educate and lead. Joseph felt a great love and respect for the man he raised as his own son, but he knew that ultimately Jesus was not on Earth to fulfill filial duties.

One day while working side-by-side on a project, Jesus stopped hammering and stared straight ahead, deep in thought. Joseph stole glances at his son over the next ten minutes as Jesus nodded his head in what seemed to be a silent dialogue with himself. Then Jesus picked up his hammer and laughed, long and deeply.

Joseph smiled, and said, "Let me in on the joke too, my son."

"Father, I don't know what to think. I have been talking to myself about how to tell you that I wish to leave this house and travel with friends across the countryside. I feel a burning in my heart that I must give the people of this land the good news of God, and yet I also feel pain at leaving you behind. But in this moment, I know that you wish me well and my worries are not founded. My love for you and my relief are immense. I feel all of this before even saying a word to you, and I know it to be true."

Joseph smiled and laid his hand upon Jesus' shoulder. "And so it is, my dear Jesus," he said. "And so it is."

Just like Jesus, we all have moments of inner awareness that change the possible outcomes of our life into the reality of living our divine plan on Earth. Grow your will and intention like wildflowers in a garden: plant the seeds of potential, nurture them with love, and watch your greatness burst forth. Let your now-moments expand and become a now-life in alignment with your higher spirit-self and God.

Jesus followed his now-moments and allowed them to transform his path in this world. Follow your own now-moments of clarity by pausing when you receive divine guidance, and really understand and feel the thoughts, sensations, and feelings flowing through you. Take a moment to truly hear the intent of the message and write it down in a "now-moment" journal. Follow it to the best of your ability. Seek clarity through automatic writing when you don't understand the message. Have courage to step into the divine realm of possibilities and live in this now-moment of existence.

5

Step Three:
Disconnecting from
Conventional Wisdom

"**J**ESUS loves me this I know, for the Bible tells me so," says an old children's song. Many of us have grown up with this reasoning for Jesus' love of humankind. This simple song bases belief in Jesus on stories in the Bible rather than on the real experience of connecting with and knowing the love of God through our own heart and mind. The Bible, religious leaders, the media, community leaders, friends, and family members tell you many things about living in the world, setting up explicit and implicit rules for functioning in society. These cultural norms make up the conventional wisdom that so many of us follow.

Jesus knew and experienced the conventional wisdom of his day as a Jew in a Roman-occupied state. He had to live under Jewish law as well as Roman law. Prophets of his day were often-times classified as heretics and madmen preaching outside of the accepted doctrines of religion. He knew that he would have to buck the conventional wisdom that said God was above and separate from humans to remind the ancient Israelites of their internal and very present connection with God. The common wisdom of Jesus' day portrayed God as a righteous deity, avenging great wrath upon enemies by forcing fires across the landscape, and only smiling upon those who abided by the strict laws of purity. Jesus presented a very different God: a benevolent being with whom all humans could connect. A father who loves his children so much that he gave them the world. A God who never forgets his wayward sheep and forgives all transgressions. Through the teachings of Jesus, God as the great father of lost souls replaced God as the great judger of the righteous followers of the old ritualistic laws of purification. Religion could no longer be exclusive, based on the laws of man, but instead became inclusive, based on the laws of God's love for all humans.

Jesus encouraged people to look past conventional thoughts about acceptance of others in society. All of his actions demonstrated a new way of living in the light of God's truth. That divine light shone harshly upon conventional behaviors that undermined the spirit of God's creations. His parables, teachings, and calculated actions showed people how to transcend the mundane thinking of the world and live from a higher place of consciousness.

Jesus turned these ancient conventions of judgment around and grounded them in love, acceptance, and forgiveness. And in doing so, he presented three powerful teaching tools, which are chronicled in the Bible, for overturning the tables of conventional wisdom. These tools shift our thinking about the workings of society and living a conventional life. If you choose the path of Spirit, these old teaching tools take on new meaning for disconnecting from judgment and accepting others with compassion and love. These three teaching tools are as follows:

- ✢ The meek shall inherit the Earth.
- ✢ The wealthy do not hold greater favor with God.
- ✢ The temple of God is not outside of us, but within us.

The Meek Shall Inherit the Earth

Everywhere he went, Jesus preached that the laws of men were stifling hearts and overshadowing the laws of God. In ancient times, people had to follow strict rules for living to remain pure in the eyes of the Jewish church. But in God's eyes, all humans are pure because they are created through the power of his love. Using that premise, Jesus held up the misfits of the world and reminded us that all of God's creations have an honored place in society. Healing their afflictions of disease and emotional pain, Jesus showed us that misfits are just people carrying a burden. Remove the burden, and the misfit becomes fit enough to enter society.

In his teachings, Jesus used the metaphor of the meek inheriting the Earth as a way to overturn society's favoritism of those who embody convention. A weak misfit represents a person who is unable to effectively shoulder the pains of life and fit into society. They cannot hide their burdens as well as others apparently can. What separates the misfits from the fit is the ability to live with pain and still function in society. Misfits remind us of the physical, emotional, and mental toll that fear places upon the human spirit. Misfits represent what a life of separation can do to us all. We are not so different from the misfits in that we all have experienced the pain of life. But it is often the weak and broken who reach out first to know God in their life, and in doing so, they inherit the abundance of divine healing power available to us all.

The Wealthy Do Not Hold Greater Favor with God

Jesus taught his followers that the material possessions of life, so desirable in ancient society, are useless in the kingdom of God. In the Bible, the rich man is told that to enter heaven, he must give away his possessions. The man refuses and admits defeat in gaining admittance.

The trappings of the conventional world are so alluring, and yet it takes more than the collection or distribution of riches to see the kingdom of God right here, right now. By accepting the great abundant world of God that exists right now, we can let go of the inessential in living a truly abundant life. To Jesus, abundance was rooted in loving and accepting others. To the rich man, abundance was rooted in loving his possessions. If he shifted his perception and the focus of his energy, the man could share his greatest gift with others: love. Instead, he chose the conventional belief that material riches hold the greatest value in life. A man doesn't give up anything to enter heaven. A man must only love more, give more, see more, and accept more of the world around him to see heaven right now. By moving his perception of abundance beyond the limited focus of monetary achievement, he would tap into even greater abundance, which may be expressed as material possessions, as well as greater love and connection with others. Spiritual abundance can be actualized in many ways, from money to love to power to friendship to faith. Old conventions limited this abundance to material wealth, which precluded many ancient people from tapping into the far greater world of spiritual wealth. Jesus taught people to see beyond the physical and look for the deeper, richer spiritual meaning of life.

The Temple of God Is Not Outside of Us but Within Us

In the Bible, Jesus is shown in the temple overturning the tables of money-changers and vendors. In ancient Jerusalem, the temple was controlled by the Romans, who employed Jewish elders to oversee the religious life of the Jews. The building held many rooms, and their functions were intricately linked with the conventions of Jewish life. To get to the main inner sanctuary of the temple, people had to pass through different chambers related to their social class and gender. Most would never reach the inner realms of the building, effectively limiting their connection with God. Only the holiest of temple elders could enter certain inner rooms that represented the closest link with God.

The temple represents an external view of our relationship

with God. Like a building with closed access, we perceive our connection with God as limited, because we can't see him. Like a hidden room, he becomes a distant part of our lives, and instead we focus on the daily grind of survival. When we forget our inner divine connection, the holy temple is no longer a sanctuary to know God. A temple of worship is not an external place when you are connected with Spirit. When you live through the power of Spirit, you become a holy vessel and temple of God. Jesus reminds us that the inner temple, the inner connection with God, is more important than the external trappings of the conventional world.

Through these three teaching tools, Jesus contradicted the values of the conventional world where the strong triumph over the weak, the rich conquer and hold all, and exclusivity is a part of praising God. In the new world of Jesus, the meek find a healing God, love holds more value than material riches, and our inner connection with God makes each of us a holy temple. To know and live these truths, Jesus began journeying out into the world to practice love, compassion, and acceptance among the people.

Shortly after his conversation with Joseph, Jesus set out on his journey of teaching others and reminding them of their internal link with God. He started out slowly, meeting with small groups of people and gently laying a foundation for bringing forth the messages of God. Jesus traveled with a few friends who had similar interests in spreading the good news of God's presence in our world. They would stay at the homes of mutual friends, meeting new people and strengthening their delivery of the messages of God. Even in these early journeys, Jesus raised concerns among those who enforced the standards of convention.

One evening while resting after a long day's walk, Jesus sat by the fire, enjoying the smell of cooking meat and a cool drink in his hand. Suddenly the door burst open, and a boy ran into the room.

Breathless, the boy asked, gasping, "Who among you is called Jesus?"

Jesus stood and motioned for the boy to sit next to him by the fire. "Tell me, young friend, what brings you here in such distress?"

The other men in the room gathered around the hearth to hear the boy speak. "The Romans are searching houses for taxes, and they have heard that Jesus has been collecting gold at his gatherings."

A murmur of dissension arose among the men. Jesus lifted up a hand to silence the group.

"I heard you speak yesterday, and I know this isn't true. I warn you to leave this house tonight, for the Romans will not be kind to you whether or not they find gold among your belongings," said the boy.

Jesus placed a hand upon the boy's shoulder. "I thank you for your help, young friend. God has sent you to us tonight, and you have done his bidding." Jesus placed his hand upon the boy's chest. "I feel the heart of God beating strong within you. Remember this feeling always."

The boy smiled as Jesus told the men to gather their things. One of the men asked why they were running from the Romans if they had God's truth on their side.

"There is a time for all things. Now is the time to walk, and one day there will be a time to stand," he replied.

"But why don't you stand up to the Romans now and show them that you have nothing to hide?"

Jesus put his hand on the man's shoulder. "In this world, truth does not always hold importance over the value of money. You and I know the truth, we know that we have nothing to hide, but these men presume us guilty before they even enter. We have much work to do now, and later we shall address the issue of what I am doing with the people."

"And what are you doing if you run at the slightest of fights?" asked the man angrily.

"I am not here to fight or prove that I am a loyal citizen. I am here to change hearts and help people to remember the God of their hearts. Nothing more, nothing less."

The Heart of the Urban Warrior

Jesus experienced life among ancient urban warriors vying for monetary gains. Romans ruled the day, often stealing, cheating, and killing for money from the poverty-stricken population of their empire. The aspiration for wealth and status existed in those days too, and the threat of expulsion from the physical world for merely blocking the way of a warrior was evident by the many crucifixions in Jerusalem.

Jesus also encountered other types of urban warriors, including closed hearts operating on autopilot, hoarders of resources, elite rulers exacting judgment over others, brute enforcers acting upon others' orders, and hiders from life. In the world of convention, these urban warriors were accepted in ancient society, but we may better recognize them by calling them the followers, the financers, the leaders, the fighters, and the runners. Each type of urban warrior is playing defense against some perceived threat, and others in the world do not matter when the alarm of fear rings. The warriors go into action, separating themselves from potential harm by any means possible.

The warriors of yesterday still exist in our world today. The pursuit of money, status, and power still drives the urban warrior, but since the ancient practice of killing others is no longer acceptable, "kill or be killed" plays out in other ways when we feel threatened. Instead we will separate, dominate, or eliminate the threat. This conventional reasoning becomes an unconscious motivator for our actions. We can live on alert, afraid that others are out to get us. We can lash out in an effort to hold on to what's ours. The final outcome of the threat event is a need to separate ourselves from others and a feeling that we can only trust ourselves to do right in this world.

The automatic responses of a convention-driven life tell us that it's okay to hurt others if you perceive them as a threat. Righteous indignation is a conventional way of responding to those whom we see as different or out of the mainstream. We can ride our high horses our entire lives, never stepping down to take a clear look at what frightens us. Jesus got off the horse and invited others to walk with him and discover a new way of living together in peace without the driving fear of separation.

Hear now as Jesus explains the road of the urban warrior:

The world turns around, always growing and changing. And yet our human race has been slow in evolving into a species of peace. Today as you reconnect with your higher spirit-self, you have the opportunity to usher in a new way of being on Earth. Rather than being guided by the past, look for guidance from the moment of who you really are. In the divine, all things are possible. It is possible to move beyond the pain of society's warriors and become warriors for peace. No longer will you suffer in isolation. Today you will release the bonds of suffering and become one with the divine world of peace, love, and harmony. There is strength in casting off the old and uniting with the new. Patience, dear one, for you have all that you need within you to complete this journey. Join me, modern-day warrior, in the pursuit of peace.

We become urban warriors when we feel the need to protect ourselves. Urban warriors let down their shields of angry words, defensive gestures, and intimidation when they realize that the action of love is greater than the reaction of separation. We have used separation as a defense for centuries, and it still doesn't work. Unity of broken hearts takes place when we realize that the threat cannot truly hurt us as eternal beings. Instead, we can accept the gift of growth and reconnection each experience offers.

As a master teacher, Jesus used parables as a way to demonstrate how change and growth are possible by learning through the experience or story of another person. Look deeply at the following story and see if a part of you lies within the lesson.

The Urban Warrior

Jack lived in a beautiful house in the suburbs of San Francisco with his lovely wife, Anna, and their two children. Jack had worked hard to become a successful computer technology entrepreneur, and his bank account identified him as a man who had everything. He owned beautiful art, acquired from the finest of collections, and he had everything a man could desire.

But Jack was far from fulfilled. He worked long hours and only saw his family on Sundays. Rarely, if ever, did he attend church with them, choosing instead to watch sports and meet them later for brunch. He said that he didn't see God in the dollar, and he would only trust in himself to get ahead in the world.

One Sunday as he watched television, he felt a dull pain in his head. He stood up to get an aspirin to relieve the pain, but he immediately felt dizzy and collapsed back onto the couch. Not used to feeling weak, he angrily tried to hoist himself up to get to the bathroom. Instead, his knees buckled and he felt a throbbing pain in his chest.

At age forty-three, he still thought of himself as a young man, still in the prime of his life. Sliding down to the floor onto his back, he stared up at his expensively frescoed ceiling. He had worked hard to attain everything in his life, and here was God's payback to him.

"Is this your kind of a joke, God?" he whispered, pain radiating down his arm. "Don't let it end like this. I'll do anything—I'll go to church, I'll donate money to the Vatican, I'll help the homeless. But please, don't let it end. Don't let me die."

At that moment, Jack heard footsteps in the hallway. Maria, the housekeeper, entered the room, grocery bags in her arms. Seeing Jack, she stopped short, dropping the bags. Running to his side, she took his hand and felt for a pulse.

"Mister Jack, do you need me to call for help?"

Jack felt gratitude and shame at the same time for being found lying on the floor, making deals with God. He mumbled for Maria to help him to sit up. Taking deep breaths, he could feel the pain lessening. Maria left his side to get him some water. Taking the cup, he held it in both shaking hands and drank.

"Maybe God is telling you something, Mister Jack," Maria said quietly.

Not looking at her, Jack whispered, "And what might that be?"

"To slow down and see the beauty that surrounds you," she said, compassion in her eyes.

Jack turned away, tears flowing down his cheeks.

Urban Myths of Separation

We've all heard of urban myths, legends of things that may or may not have happened. Like the story of the young couple making out in a car parked in a secluded area, who hear a scratching noise on the door and drive off in a hurry only to later find a deadly hook hanging from the door handle. We all shiver, saying that could never happen, and yet we secretly wonder if this could have been based on a true story.

Our lives follow the patterns of many urban myths, and often we don't recognize that we base our values on the antiquated social mores of our ancestors. We spend our lives honoring relatives who have transitioned back to the divine realm, oftentimes missing out on developing our own path in the world and forging new avenues of living. Our life can be mapped out by others, based on accepted patterns of behavior in society. Women can easily bear children and become the matriarch of a family. Men can easily become the breadwinner and the patriarch of the family. We look to the standards set by our parents, grandparents, and fictional families that are popularized and idealized as the standard of society. Based on these old conventions, we set limited ideals that we strive to attain.

We may fulfill our physical destiny as parents, our occupational destiny through a career, but we can miss out on attaining our spiritual destiny because we are afraid to look at how separate we feel from our inner self and God. Jesus gave us a blueprint for becoming spiritual masters, but our conventional wisdom has superceded this innate power within us. It's like holding a key in your hand, but not realizing it's there because you don't see a door in front of you that needs opening. Societal mores are like bushes growing over and blocking the doorway. You need to do a little brush clearing before you can use your inner keys to open up to a new standard of behavior. You have to take all that you know and be willing to push it out of the way to move beyond the urban myths of separation.

Jesus experienced the effects of these myths two thousand years ago. He knew that by traveling the countryside and preaching the good news of God, he was setting up himself and his family for ridicule and resentment. Prophets were judged harshly and revered by few. Their followers were viewed as zealots on the bottom rung of society. Jesus was telling people about the kingdom of God, whose existence required faith in an unseen world. He was asking people of a society based on fear, brutality, and scarcity to lay down their defense shield of urban myths and give into their unconscious desires for spirituality. Many chose to kill the messenger rather than hear the message.

Despite the pain these urban myths have caused, we still know the words of Jesus' message. Many of his disciples wrote down his teachings in some form, adding or subtracting parts of his message. Even though we did not get to see him teach with our own eyes, the heart of his message is contained in the Bible. Reading the Bible through the lens of love and compassion, we are reminded to:

- Give love, and you will receive love.
- Have faith, and you will know God.
- Forgive your neighbor, and your heart will be healed.
- Accept your divine path, and you will live in heaven upon Earth.

Urban myths have evolved over the centuries, but their effects continue. They counteract the teachings of Jesus. Through the life of Jesus, God gave us a key to finding the meaning of life. Some have followed this quest, while others have developed societal mores to keep the illusion of separation intact. Urban myths twist and shield the greatness of Jesus' divine messages and imply that by following these teachings, we will experience separation from self, others, and God in these ways:

+ Give love, and your heart will be broken.
+ Have faith, and you open yourself to disappointment by God.
+ Forgive your neighbor, and he will offend you again.
+ Accept your divine path, and you will live in isolation from the rest of society.

We all have swords and mythic defense shields that keep us separate from others and God. We use others' actions in society to justify our own reasons for buying into these urban myths of separation. At a certain point, these myths become an unconscious part of our decision-making process. We become afraid to take chances, to step out of the so-called comfort zone provided by societal values. We become hidden in the landscape of society, perpetuating these myths through our choice to remain separate and safe from the perceived dangers of life.

Hear now as Jesus explains the process for breaking free from conventional wisdom to live the life you truly desire:

Dear ones, I know how closely you follow the conventions of your time. You know at what age to do certain things, and how successful you should be at each activity. You become trapped on the game board of life, fearing what will happen if you stop playing the game and think for yourself. Take my hand, and I will guide you back to your own divine wisdom. Your higher spirit-self exists in a world without pain and strife. This being is you. Peace is yours because you already hold it within your essence. Release the bondage of society's conventions, and you tap into something much greater: God's truth. And this is the truth that allows you to do your divine work here on Earth. You are here for a reason. Awake and do your part to bring peace to Earth.

Urban myths lull us into accepting conventions at face value. In the world of Jesus, we look closely at each myth through the lens of love. If you examine a myth through the lens of judgment, fear, or scarcity, you're entrapped by circular logic, because the myth was originally created to separate us from the perceived threat of judgment, fear, or scarcity. Wrap the myth in love and compassion, and your inner wisdom will guide you to a new standard of behavior based on living in the light of truth.

Courage to See through God's Eyes

"Take my hand, Jesus," said his angel one night while he lay awake. He had been traveling for many days and felt tired, and yet he couldn't sleep. His angel had suddenly appeared before him, and he did as he was asked.

Instantly he felt as if his soul was lifted out of his body. Pulled along by his angel, he moved quickly through a whirling haze of colors until they stopped in an ethereal cave. Water dripped from the ceiling, forming a pool on the ground. The angel motioned for Jesus to sit in the water. The cool water immediately sated his thirst though none had passed through his lips. A ring of fire suddenly appeared around the pool, and Jesus could feel it heating the water.

The water quickly grew warm and was soon boiling. But Jesus sat peacefully despite the inferno raging around him. Through the steam, he could see God approaching him. God sat down in the water, facing Jesus.

"See the world through my eyes, dear Jesus," said God as he bent forward and touched his forehead to Jesus'. A multitude of images flashed before Jesus' eyes. He saw women dancing, their whirling skirts flowing and suddenly becoming capes blowing against the legs of men riding camels. The legs of the camels moved slowly back and forth until the image turned into a child, sitting on the ground waving a stick back and forth in the air. The stick disappeared and the child's arms were waving from a basket, trying to reach his mother. The bending figure of the mother changed into the dancer again, undulating up and down to the music.

God sat back, and the final image faded. "You have seen the universe flowing into my being. I see all, I hear all, I am the keeper of all. These multitudes of experience dwell within my being, forever changing and growing. You have seen the world through God's eyes, and you shall let it forever change the way you live in the world."

Jesus sat up, again in his earthly bed. His angel stood before him.

"You have felt the glance of God, lived within his world. You have seen the flow of the universe, felt its power and movement. God is energy, nothing more, nothing less. Knowing this, you will have the strength to walk the divine path in a savage world," she said.

Just as Jesus did, you see the physical world around you. Its rhythms lull you into a sleeping state of living. Seeing the energy of God, and letting it touch and move through you, awakens you to a new world of possibilities. In this new world, pain and fear lose their dominance, shifting our belief system away from conventional wisdom. When you act from a place of love, you are not behaving within the general standards of the conventional world. We all strive to be more loving, but most of our conventions are based on separation from self, others, and God. Letting go of the illusions of life is one of the first steps Jesus took to attain a greater connection with his inner wisdom.

Letting God's eyes become your own changes how you view the world and its illusions of pain. But when you have cut your finger, it's hard to say that pain is an illusion. When you have cried tears over a failed relationship, it's hard to say that pain is an illusion. When you start a new path that others may not understand, it's hard to say that pain is an illusion. Life is about letting go of the illusions and coming to terms with who you really are: a divine being having a human experience. In believing this realization, you can see how you have bought into the obstacles of life. Conventional wisdom, limited thinking, fears of change, chains binding you to outdated social mores—all of these obstacles keep you thinking that you are merely a human being having a very human experience. In accepting your eternal connection with God and your inner wisdom, you broaden your horizons and expand your expectations for a greater life. You step out of the box of the old world and into a new realm of divine living.

One of the first steps to letting go of conventional illusions is determining how you weigh in on the scale of conventional norms. Where does your mark fall on the measuring stick of society? Are you conventional, following a set path in life that's been charted by millions before you? Are you a maverick, bucking old ways for the adventurous path? Or are you a lost soul, not quite certain of where you belong, and just getting by day to day? Even these labels are set up by society to classify you and give you security that you either fit into society or can expect to be rejected by society. Either way, you know your place.

So how do you look at your present situation without using societal labels to define your place in the world? Take it up one step: you are a divine being having a human experience on Earth. Nothing more, nothing less. When you realize that you are here for the experience, you can begin to step back from the sting of societal conventions. If you are here for the experience, you can choose to have a painful experience or a growth experience. It's your choice, not the choice of society around you. If you live it, you will become it. It's as simple as that. If you live in peace, you are peace.

Jesus learned this lesson through seeing the world through God's eyes.

Listen now as Jesus explains how the universal flow of energy supports our growth:

Dear ones, God holds all experiences of the Earth realm within his being. He functions as the creator force of the universe. This energy supports growth as well as destruction, for all energy comes from the divine realm and returns to the divine realm. Energy moves constantly, shifting and changing. You are made of this energy. It is within your nature to change and grow. You are a divine being having a human experience to continue the relentless pursuit of experience.

So how can you live in peace when you may not feel that you know how to find that essence within? Many saints have pondered this question. Saint Augustine wondered how to find peace in a world where hatred and poverty of soul seemed so pervasive. And yet he was able to look beyond the physical manifestations of fear, the vengeful actions of people, and find that peace lies just below the surface of pain. At the moment of impact of an action, a simple choice is made by the participants to react in fear or react with peace. It's the realization that you have a choice, that you can control your response in the moment that allows you to find the peace within your essence.

Remembering your free will, your choice to react in the moment, frees you from the chains of society. Seize the moment and make it yours, molding your response to reflect the peace and divinity within your being. Know that throwing stones upon another person that you perceive has injured you has been done for thousands of years. Society teaches the Old Testament "eye for an eye" maxim, which encourages you to avenge harm against you. In the divine moment of your response, know that peace lies within you. You have felt it before. Let it guide you in the moment to calmly state your peace without harming another being's free will. We cannot control others through fear and other conventions of separation. We can only influence them through peace.

Practice reaching down into the peace well within you by using the following affirmation from Jesus. He used this affirmation to help center himself before interacting and teaching among the people. He chose to see all people as God's children, united in love and peace. This choice set the tone for all of his interactions with others, and it had the power to override the energy of convention around him. Others would unconsciously react based on societal mores. Jesus consciously chose peace, which would shift the interaction to a higher level, requiring the sleeping warriors to wake up and participate in the new situation. Active, awake, and questioning are good states of being for releasing the bonds of conventional wisdom.

I Am the Peace of the Universe Affirmation

I am the peace of the universe.
I am the wholeness of the world.
I am the freedom of the wind.
I am the movement of the trees.
I am the flight of the bird.
I am the cry of the child.
I am the energy of his cells.
I am the peace of the universe.
Peace dwells within and around me.
I open my peace to myself and to all around me.
Peace be within you.

Using the Christ Wisdom Framework

Jesus found through his journey to awakening that the heart of God beat strongly within his being. As he reclaimed his divine heritage and let go of old societal illusions, he found that he also burned brightly within, shining forth the light of God from his being. This light was tangible, a strong personal power that was felt by those around him and by those who heard tales of his teachings.

When we step back from living a conventional life, we tap into a more abundant source for living: our personal power. By reconnecting with the God of our hearts, we link into the power of Spirit. Spirit flows with love, abundance, hope, faith, joy, and peace, and these energies become the basis for our actions and behavior. These loving energies are not always present in our interactions with others, and we notice when we are touched by their grace. Jesus exuded this personal power when he taught among the people, and he turned many angry hearts to peace.

Just as Jesus reclaimed his personal power, you too can link back into your inner greatness and move in love and peace through the world. Disconnecting from conventional wisdom may leave you wondering how to interact with others. Our set conventions for behavior in society provide a framework, but oftentimes we are strangled by their hold on our lives. Break the hold and you feel free, though perhaps somewhat lost as to how to make your way through the world.

Using the Christ wisdom framework, you can learn to work within a divine structure developed by you, your higher spirit-self, and God. Jesus chose to develop a framework of love, which was a specific energetic way to interact with other beings that respected his own mastery and the mastery of others. He chose to treat others with candor and respect, not hiding behind the convention of never addressing what is truly going on in a situation. Jesus dropped all pretenses and spoke the truth, refusing the conventions of duplicity.

How can you let your personal power shine forth and light your way along the divine path? Use Jesus' framework as a model for developing your own code of behavior based on love, forgiveness, acceptance, and peace.

Developing the Christ Wisdom Framework

1. Release yourself from the bonds of conventional wisdom. When you feel the pressures of society influencing your behavior and actions, consciously say, *I willingly release the conventions of society.*

2. Ask for divine guidance in creating your own divine framework of wisdom. Connect with your higher spirit-self, and ask for a new standard of behavior and code of actions based on love and acceptance of others. Listen quietly, and write down this new wisdom.

3. Live in love based on this new code of behavior. Fear not how others will view you. Always act from a place of love by being honest about your motivations. Never hide who you are. Only seek to reveal to others the truth of your being.

Jesus developed this framework as he continued his travels around ancient Israel. He progressed from teaching small groups of people to talking to larger gatherings outside of temples. Jesus mainly taught outside of temples because he believed that God's wisdom was for all, and not just for the people of one religion. As he grew in personal power, he would share this loving energy with others as they gathered to hear him speak.

One day Jesus entered the courtyard of a large temple where many people were waiting for him. He walked to the center of the crowd, scanning the beings surrounding him with his inner eyes. Some men had red energy fields that rose high above them, while others had small, brown fields. The angry and the sick always attended his talks, which pleased him. He wanted to reach out and help these people to release the energies blocking their true essences.

He also saw people with blue and purple energy fields, which showed their desire to learn and connect with the God energy within. Others had bright green fields. These people were often eager to join forces with Jesus and help heal the wounds of the beings around them.

That day, Jesus noticed that many in the crowd had red and black energy fields. He felt the presence of anger and violence in the gathering. He did not fear this energy, however, because he knew that his response to it could dissipate or exacerbate the tension around him. He chose to actively address the feelings of the crowd. He had found on his journeys that just by naming the energy around him, he could change and move it toward peace.

He felt his higher spirit-self envelop him as he spoke. "My

friends, today I join you to tell you about the good news of God. And yet I feel that some here do not join me with a lightness of heart. I feel pain here, anger, sadness, disbelief. I am not asking you to set aside your own beliefs, only to take a moment to hear mine. I share my beliefs with you through love and only ask that you receive this message with the love intended behind it."

He scanned the crowd again with his inner eyes. He watched as the red energy turned to pink, a sign of love. But some held onto their anger, rigid and unmoving. Jesus raised his hands and held them over the crowd.

"Let us begin with a blessing. Blessed be our God, our creator of the world. Blessed be his name, holy and true. Blessed be his creations, his people of this world. Blessed be his children, for the fruit of his labors are ripe and full. Blessed be you, for you and I share this bond with our father. Bless you, my brothers and sisters, as I begin to share with you the good news of God for today."

As he looked at the crowd, he now saw only one man with a black energy field, tinged with red. Looking straight at him, Jesus silently blessed him, but his field remained the same. Knowing that this was the man's choice, he continued to give his talk in love.

Peace Shields in the Valley of Death

Living without pretense can feel like walking through the valley of the shadow of death without protection. Our lives can be so chaotic, full of pain and strife, and if we drop our defenses of judgment and anger, we wonder if we will be hurt by others who still carry these swords. Jesus stripped himself of his old defenses, but he did not run bare through the world, open to injury. Instead, he donned the peace shields of a warrior acting from a place of truth and honor, never allowing others to tread over him. A warrior of the heart is a messenger of peace, a gladiator for truth, an emissary of love. Place the robes of love, peace, harmony, faith, hope, and forgiveness upon your being, and you will never walk the path alone.

As Jesus began to establish himself as a man of God, he found it difficult sometimes not to feel attacked by those who did not agree with him. His detractors would speak vehemently and critically. Often he would have to release self-doubt when others would insist that he was a heretic and should keep his opinions to himself.

One day after a man spoke to him in a cruel, demeaning way, Jesus retreated to the hills for some quiet, contemplative time. He sat down among three boulders, resting his back against one. He breathed deeply for many minutes, slowly releasing the pain of the interaction and reestablishing divine order and balance within his being.

As peace once again pervaded his body, he felt the presence of God near him. Opening his eyes, he could see a large bird perched on one of the rocks.

"I fly free through the heavens," the bird of God said to his inner ears. "I am beauty. I am life everlasting. I hold your heart within mine. I hold the heart of all within me. When I soar through the heavens, I bring a piece of you within me. When I am sore below the heavens, I bring the peace of you within me."

Jesus smiled at the bird. After a moment he said, "Take my pain away, dear one, wash me of my doubt. Let me always know that I am one with my brother. Let me remember the pain of doubt and not let it cloud my vision of the divine within my brother."

"Always remember that your brother chooses his mask," replied the bird. "See the mask for what it is. Let not the words of a shield penetrate your heart. Hear the words only in love. Wrap your love around the words, and the sting will not touch your heart."

Jesus sat silently with the bird, watching the sun lower in the sky.

6

Step Four:
Operating from a Higher Source

"WALK with me, my friend, and I will show you the way of peace," said the ascended master to the inner ears of Jesus. Jesus stood up beside the tree under which he had been meditating. He laid his hand upon the arm of the glowing master, who led him deeper into the wilderness.

"Master, why is it that you look real to me?" Jesus asked. "I can see your body, your robes, your hair, and even your arm seems solid to me."

The master stopped walking and turned to face Jesus, placing his hand upon Jesus' shoulder. "You feel real to me too. And yet I know that inside of that shell of yours, a strong force of energy is waiting to be released. You hide your fluidity well within your body. I only borrowed this shell so that I may be with you on Earth today."

With that, the master turned and continued walking. Jesus studied the master's back as he walked behind him. He could see little bursts of golden energy rising up from the master, and a white glow surrounded his body. As the master crossed the top of a knoll and disappeared behind a boulder, Jesus hurried to catch up.

As he passed the boulder, Jesus saw the master sitting in a clearing. He motioned for Jesus to sit beside him. Jesus settled down comfortably in front of the master and looked at him expectantly. The master reached into his robe and pulled out a viper. Jesus' eyes widened as the master placed the snake on the ground between them. The snake hissed and coiled upon itself, glaring menacingly at Jesus. He did not take his eyes from the snake as the master began to speak.

"You see before you an enemy, a being who could take life from you in one strike. You fear his power, his ability to make you cower and run from his presence," said the master. He paused, waiting for a reaction from Jesus.

Across from him, Jesus sat very still, looking into the eyes of the snake. He knew the words of the master were true, and yet he could not acknowledge them. He would have run if he could, but he knew his movement would cause the snake to strike. With great effort, he raised his eyes to meet the master's.

The master smiled, and whispered, "Watch."

The master lifted his hands over the viper. The snake hissed and turned toward the master. Jesus did not move as the master started chanting to the snake, filling the clearing with a low melodious sound. Using his inner eyes, Jesus could see a pink energy flowing from the master's hands and enveloping the snake. The snake slowly unfurled itself and slithered toward a bush, disappearing into the undergrowth.

Jesus looked at the master, who had folded his hands into his lap. He wondered what else might be lurking within his robes.

The master laughed and stood with amazing speed. "I do not need this form any longer," he said. The edges of his body blurred, and Jesus could see tiny bits of energy breaking off and buzzing around his form. The master quickly disintegrated into a million little pieces, illuminating the clearing.

"I am peace when I give peace to others. No being can hurt me when I am love. I have no fear when I do not allow fear in my being. Even the poison of a million vipers cannot bear witness to my demise when I give in to the glory of my being," said the master, who now appeared as a soft glowing light in front of Jesus.

Jesus stood and reached out to the master, and his hand was enfolded by light. He could feel the warm energy encircling his hand, tingling upon his skin.

"Show me this peace within," Jesus said.

The light of the master enveloped Jesus, and he could feel emotions rising within his body. A calmness, an assuredness of soul, a compassion unparalleled, a faith unwavering, a love unbridled, and a humility unbounded coursed through his being. A great knowingness spread through Jesus, and he knew that he had felt this peace before.

He turned to see the snake emerging from the bush. He could see the red energy emanating from it as it slithered toward him. Raising his hands, he let the love of his being flow forth and envelop the snake. It advanced quickly toward him, unrelenting.

Jesus began singing a blessing to the snake, "My brother, my love for you is complete, my compassion for you is great. Together we walk this Earth, brothers united by our maker. I honor you and let you pass in peace."

The snake slowed its progression and veered on its path. It slowly slid past Jesus and disappeared into the brush.

Jesus turned to the master, whose glowing energy floated beside him.

"Only in love may we truly face our enemy of fear, dear Jesus."

Using the Wisdom of the Divine

In this section, you will meet and experience different lessons with saints, masters, and angels, just as Jesus did upon his journey. Let these divinely inspired meditations, affirmations, and visualizations act as a springboard to your own inner work with these beings, as well as with your own personal divine guides. As you read about each guide, sense how they must have felt when serving humanity in an earthly or divine capacity. Let this commitment to service inspire you to step out of the everyday world and into the new world of assisting yourself and others through the power of Spirit.

In our everyday world, we forget about the mysteries of life. Saints, masters, and angels remind us of the wonders of our universe, showing us that there is more to this world than the physical features we recognize. We have access to the great creator energy of God to create our own experiences. We know this energy as creativity, and we use it to create beautiful paintings, flowing words that inspire others, and functional objects to ease our way through this world. We also use our creativity to create inner worlds of pain, such as awful scenarios in which we are hurt by others. We choose how to use our creative force, and connecting with saints, masters, and angels puts us on the path to aligning this power with God's creator energy. Miracles happen when you ask God to help you to remember how to use this creative energy to serve yourself and humanity.

Connecting with the Saints

Through his own inner work, Jesus connected with many divine beings who we today would call saints. Saints have been recognized by religious organizations as people who have made significant contributions to the physical, emotional, mental, and spiritual well-being of humanity. Compassion, faith, loyalty, love, humility, truth, and service to others characterize these beings, who showed us by example how to awaken spiritually and become instruments of God. Like Jesus, these saints were not superhuman but rather courageous beings who bucked conventional wisdom and had the strength to lead others by listening to and following their own inner guidance.

In calling them saints, we tend to set these men and women above us on the scale of leading a Spirit-driven life. But if you remove the label of saint, all that sets these individuals apart from us is their great courage and faith. We all are born with the capacity to do wondrous things through the power of Spirit. All it takes is a momentary leap into the unknown, because the instant you enter the unfamiliar, it becomes known again. Like Jesus, saints give us a roadmap to divinity, a path to walk upon to achieve the same great spiritual accomplishments.

Mother Teresa

Mother Teresa is the most recent saint to pass through the veil to the divine. She never considered herself to be anything beyond a servant of God, and yet she demonstrated to millions of modern-day people an unbounded compassion for humanity. She worked with people others would turn from. She sought to comfort the downtrodden, not through pity, but by showing them the love God holds in his heart for them. In lifting up others through love, Mother Teresa gave them wings to soar through life.

Hear now as Mother Teresa shares her wisdom for spreading God's love:

My dear ones, I have only but left you, but my love for you continues. I soar above you now, and you may not feel my hand upon your skin, but I gently carry your burdens for you still. On Earth, the pain can seem so intense, so blinding to the world around you. You feel down, low to the Earth, filled with despair. I have held your hand, reminded you of God's great love for you. I hope that I have sparked a place within you that desires to reach out to others and fill them with your abundance of love. Love, peace, and compassion—those were all that I needed to do my work. And the loving hand of Jesus, guiding me along my path. I listened daily to his wisdom for me, always saying, "More, what more can I do? Let me know how I can help and do your work, Lord. Let me be your hands to touch the world as you would have." Be the hands of God, let his love flow freely from you, and serve your brothers and sisters as he wishes you to. I bless you with peace, my dear ones. Know that I am always near, close by to hear your prayers and help you in any way that I can.

Mother Teresa lived during the modern age, and yet she was able to cast aside the modern afflictions of indifference and preoccupation with material success to help those around her. One thing Mother Teresa demonstrated to us all is that the work of God can be done here on Earth today. You may not have the same calling as Mother Teresa, but you do have a mission that is just as valuable. Learn from this selfless woman how to open your heart to the divine within by using her personal meditation technique.

Divine Purpose Meditation

Find a quiet spot to sit, preferably in a darkened room. As you make yourself comfortable, breathe deeply into your lower belly, filling yourself with the breath of life. This breath is a gift of God, and on each inhalation, breathe in the bounty of God. Say what essence of God you are breathing in, be it hope, peace, love, faith, honor, truth, integrity, or service. Take a moment to let this essence fill you, becoming this God-given moment of clarity.

Now it is time to wrap the cloth of God around you. See a cloth lying on the floor. Well-worn, used daily, this old cloth has seen many lives and felt many hands upon its fabric. Gently, lovingly, pick up the cloth of God and wrap it around your shoulders so that it completely covers your body. Feel this gentle friend lovingly embrace your body. Familiar, so comforting, this cloth of God dissolves into your body, leaving behind only a glowing light. You are now wrapped and living within God's grace.

Warm and loved, you are ready to ask what God's will is for you. Open your hands and hold them out in front of you. Say out loud, *God, let your will be known for me. What might I do to ease the way for humanity? How may I be of service to you, and my brothers and sisters?*

Now be still and listen, deep within yourself. Feel what your heart has to say to you. See the pictures or images within your mind, paying close attention to what is being communicated to you. Take the time to allow God to commune with you.

When you have heard, seen, and felt God's plan for you in this moment, lift up your hands and give thanks to the Lord.

Saint Catherine of Genoa

Hope and faith are essential to a spiritual life, truths Saint Catherine found during her life in a small Italian town in the fifteenth century. Though she found herself in a loveless marriage, as a well-bred woman of society, she continued to be the best wife she could despite the circumstances. However, one day her world was turned upside down when Jesus spoke to her, opening up an inner world of introspection and peace. Not content to keep this peace within, Saint Catherine sought to share this divine connection with the world. She wrote books about her divine revelations and opened her home to groups interested in a personal journey with the divine.

Saint Catherine could have been living today, based on her story of finding the divine during a very unlikely time of her life. She was not seeking answers, and yet the secrets of the universe revealed themselves to her. She created a personal spiritual practice as she walked her divine journey. She enjoyed nature and would use walking meditations to center herself. Use the following meditation upon your own walks to establish your link to the divine.

The Wonder of Nature Meditation

Go to a quiet, lovely spot in nature. A park, a deserted path, a quiet place in your yard. Go to a place where you feel close to the Earth, where your heart feels at peace and you know that you are a part of this universe.

As you enter your place in nature, open your eyes to the world around you. Let your glance fall upon a flower or a beautiful shrub. Look carefully at the plant, feeling its beauty become a part of your being. Inhale the plant's essence, filling yourself with the love and serenity of this living organism. Let your pace, your inner clock, be set upon the pace of the plant. Feel yourself slow down so that you become this life-form who looks to the sky for sun and rain. Feel the wind gently blow upon you, ruffling your hair, renewing your countenance.

Begin to walk slowly through this nature sanctuary. With each step you take, breathe deeply and slowly, matching your pace to your breath. Purposefully but gingerly, step through nature, feeling yourself a part of this great Earth you live upon. Your body is a celebration of sensations, and let the party begin now. Feel your face now. Notice a warm sensation from the sun, or chilly spots on your cheeks. How do your arms feel? Light and swinging or still and at peace? Notice your legs now. Are they heavy or do they feel buoyant? Take all of these sensations in, knowing that your body is a living, breathing divine vessel of God.

Now find a quiet spot to sit. Center yourself in front of a plant that speaks to your mood in this moment, be it a tree, flower, bush, weed, or shrub. Open your hands so that you can feel the energy of the plant flowing out to you. Breathe deeply, inhaling the wonder of nature, a gift of God to us.

When you feel renewed and refreshed, slowly rise and carry the wonder of this sacred place within you as you journey back into the everyday world.

Saint Michael, the Archangel

Healer, lover of humanity, provider of peace and faith, holy messenger of God—all of these words can be used to describe Saint

Michael, who has momentarily taken on human form throughout the centuries to touch the lives of humans on Earth. Saint Michael walked with the grace of God, using his energy to heal people of ailments and afflictions of the heart. His faith in God is great, and his love for humanity is immense. He has given all of himself to serve God and his brothers and sisters selflessly.

Hear now the message of Saint Michael for you:

Dear ones, let my heart speak to your heart, and know that we are one in the kingdom of God. Listen now as I share the wonders of God for your life, and the mysteries of the universe for unraveling the messages of the divine. Love, pure and simple, is all that is needed to survive and grow in this world. Love, pure and simple, heals broken hearts and lifts the forms of God's children to the light. Know that love heals energetically and can change the outlook of a dying man. Give love to the downhearted, and you have lifted a soul to heaven. Feel love within your heart, and the separation between you and others melts. Let love guide you, lift you, fill you, and be you as you journey with the divine.

The healing powers of Saint Michael are renowned, and many pray to him for his blessings. When in human form, Saint Michael would endow objects with healing powers and use them when laying hands upon people seeking relief from ailments. Use his energy meditation upon a sacred object, such as a stone, cross, crystal, ring, amulet, or any other talisman that represents love and power to you.

Sacred Object Meditation

Place your selected object upon a soft cloth, which will be used to cradle the object when the meditation is complete. This object is sacred and will be filled with the love of God. This is no idle transformation. This object will embody the essence of God's love and healing power for you. Use it well and with love for yourself and others.

Hold your hands over the object. Close your eyes and ask God to clear all energies of pain and fear from your being. See a white light surrounding your body, purifying your essence. The light dissolves into your body, giving off a soft glow. Your glowing hands will now be used to clear energies from your sacred object. Ask God to clear all energies of pain and fear from the object. Allow God to use your hands to magnify his divine energy and clear the object.

Now place your hands upon the object. Say out loud, *God, use me to fill this sacred object with love. Let me be your giver of peace and healing energy. Let me use this object for giving love and peace to all who touch it.* Keep your hands upon the object, and allow God's energy to flow through you. Keep your mind and heart open, clear of fear and worries.

When you feel the energy movement stop, place the object over your heart. Say out loud, *God, use my heart of love to christen this object with divine love and understanding. Let divine wisdom flow, imparting its essence upon this object.* Hold the object to your heart until the energy movement is complete.

Now your sacred object is energized and ready to be used for healing yourself and others through love. When using the object, hold it gently. With great respect, call upon its God energy when placing it upon others for healing. You may use phrases such as, *God, I ask your will to be known for healing this person. Let the divine love endowed in this sacred object flow freely and fully to restore divine harmony and love within this being. And so it is, upon your will.*

When not using the object, store it within the soft cloth in a safe, dry place.

Connecting with the Masters

Jesus showed his power as a master by overcoming the blindness of the human condition to access his inner greatness while here upon Earth. Ascended masters are just as the name implies: they have ascended above the fear-based thoughts and actions of human form and connected into the divine source of energy, wisdom, and love. These masters have come back to Earth many times to help lead humans on the divine path. We know them by many names and have benefited from their sharing of knowledge and divine insight.

Jesus worked within the inner realms of his being to access these masters. Through meditation, affirmations, and dream work, he connected with specific masters at different times during his journey to awaken his heart and mind to his inherent power and divinity. These masters are available to us all during our own journey, and all you need to do is invite them into your

---

conscious world to assist you in remembering the greatness of your being.

Moses

A prophet and a visionary leader, Moses united and led his people on the road to freedom. He worked within, among, and above groups of people to bring harmony and love where none existed before. He selflessly helped others on their own paths to greatness while still connecting with God on his own. He united the incongruent and mended the broken. He spoke with eloquence and passion, bringing forth the good news of God to the people of his time. He embraced his divine connection without doubt and was counted upon to tell people what they needed to hear to get moving into a new land of hope.

Listen now to the stirring words of Moses for you:

Dear ones, it is with great affection and love that I stand before you now to share this message of love from the divine world. I have been among you many times, and yet you may not have recognized me, only felt the power of the gifts I have been chosen to bestow upon you. Know that I bring you peace in your hour of darkness, that I bring the sun to your world when the light never seems to return. Know that I answer your prayers for guidance, that I hear every utterance for salvation on the path to the divine. Know that I love you with the heart of a man who once roamed the Earth, and it is with great compassion that I reach out to you now. Let down your load and allow me to release your burdens.

Moses helped Jesus often during his teachings to the people of Israel. Jesus would call upon him for wisdom and energy to do the work that needed to be done. One afternoon Jesus came upon a gathering of people outside of a temple. This crowd was not waiting for him, but he saw an opportunity to touch lives in that moment.

As he walked into the center of the group, he mentally called upon Moses to help him embody the essence of a divine uniter and leader. Moses immediately appeared by his side and began giving him guidance for opening the crowd to hear his message.

You too can learn how to unite others for the common good by using Moses' words to Jesus as an affirmation.

Unity of One Affirmation

I am one with you.
I fill my heart with love when I touch you.
I leave all differences and judgments behind.
I give you my full and undivided attention
for you are a master of this world.
I honor all that is within you
for you are a master of the divine world.

Mother Mary

It takes a master to raise a master in this world. Mary was chosen to be the mother of Jesus because she embodies divine devotion and strength. Mary was a strong young woman, and she showed exceptional character when she was called upon by God to raise Jesus. She also began her own personal journey to the divine at that moment, and she opened her own connection to her higher spirit-self and God to carry out her mission on Earth. Her love and commitment are recognized throughout the world, and many seek her guidance through prayer.

Hear now as Mother Mary shares her message of love:

My beloved ones, I share my blessings freely and fully with you, for you too are the children of God. I held Jesus in my arms, a newborn baby entering this world with an incredible mission of love for humanity. In that moment, my world changed, and I became a new person. I too shed my old burdens and sought to be the highest and best I could be for myself, my son, and my family. I reach out to you now with love and understanding, knowing that you often feel overwhelmed in this world. Know that I too once walked upon the Earth, and I understand how fully images and sounds can blind you to the divine world around you. I too had to step outside of my shell and become more than just a woman living in savage times. I became the embodiment of divinity, a vessel for the divine child. Your task, your plan from God is just as noble, for each life here is an opportunity to reconnect fully and share your gifts with others. Open up now, let down your walls of pain, and let God help you to see your true self. I see you there, feeling small, and my heart reaches out to you. I see your full abundance just below the surface, and I feel your greatness within. I know what you are capable of, and I honor you greatly.

Mother Mary meditated daily to strengthen her will and resolve to share her divinity with the world. She shares the following meditation, which was her favorite after Jesus returned to the divine realm. She missed his physical presence even though she connected with him daily through her silent time in nature. You can use the following meditation to connect with Jesus, as well as with a loved one who has passed on to the divine realm.

Beloved Connection Meditation

Find a quiet spot where you will not be disturbed. Make yourself comfortable, and begin to breathe deeply. With each breath, see white light enter your body through your crown. As the white light fills your body, old blocking energy is pushed out of your feet. Continue filling yourself until you feel cleansed and refreshed.

Now hold in your mind an image of Jesus. See a brilliant white light emanating from the body of Jesus, a vital being who is alive and full of energy. See him reach out and embrace you. Feel his touch, knowing that he is energetically in the room with you, holding you close. Let his energy enter your heart, breaking down the physical barrier between you. Embrace him fully with your essence, extending your unconditional love to meet his.

When you're ready, hold Jesus' hands and connect with him emotionally. Let him know how you are feeling in this moment. Share your feelings of love for him or any other emotions of the moment. Now ask Jesus to share his feelings for you. Let the words, images, sounds, or thoughts pour over you, allowing them to be expressed fully to you.

When you're ready, step back from Jesus. See him again surrounded by the loving light of divinity. Now allow that light to enfold you. Feel its healing power and love surge through you. Sit quietly for a moment and let it truly touch you.

To connect with a loved one, see that person standing next to Jesus. See a brilliant white light surrounding your beloved. You embrace, holding your beloved close, extending and accepting unconditional love.

When you're ready, hold your beloved's hands and connect emotionally in this moment, sharing your feelings with each other. When you're ready, step back from your beloved. See your loved one again surrounded by the loving light of God. Open your eyes, knowing that you have felt the heart of Jesus and connected with your beloved through the love and power of Jesus.

Buddha

"Do you know what lies within the heart of humanity? Do you know what lies within your own heart?" Buddha has asked many a follower.

Buddha spoke of letting go of the inessential to find the essential within. Like a mystery, the flower of the heart unfolds when you allow silence to touch your being. The silence of the encounter acts as a powerful force, stripping down the barriers to the core of your essence. Naked, unclothed of burdens, you present the real you and experience life from the bare perspective of truth. You become the divine unbridled, full and alive to the possibilities around you.

Buddhist traditionalists follow the path of least resistance, meaning they let go of old ideas rather than expending energy to keep something that is not a part of their essence. Buddha taught and continues to teach disciples on this divine path of enlightenment.

Hear now as Buddha shares his philosophy for enlightenment:

Beloved children of God, we are truly one in the energy of the divine. Stripped down to our bare essence, we all embody hope, peace, love, and faith. Forgive and forget. Release and move on. Live and laugh along the journey. Know that the illusions of life are transparent, and you may lovingly let go of them in the silence. Stop the chatter of the mind and you will remember the kernels of truth that are uniquely your own. Stop the chatter of the world around you, and you help your brothers and sisters to remember their divinity. Step out in peace, and do not sit upon your perch in enlightenment. The journey begins with you but ends with another. Share your peace in love.

Buddha used silence as a tool for easing the pain within the mind. Silence loosens the grip of the ego and allows pain to leave the conscious mind. Use the following meditation to quiet the inner critic and as a way to sit in action.

Essential Silence Meditation

Find a quiet, dimly lit room. Sit on the floor, using a cushion to comfortably brace your lower back. You may sit against a wall for support with your legs in a comfortable sitting position.

Begin by breathing very slowly and deeply. Each breath fills you with life everlasting, so take a moment to truly feel this divine gift enter your body. Feel the air enter your nostrils. Follow the breath down the throat, through the chest, and into the belly. Focus here for a few moments, fully living in this moment of breath.

Now focus on the breath as it leaves the body. Feel it slowly lift up through the belly, rush up through the throat, and out of the nostrils. Focus here for a moment, feeling the exchange of energy of exhaling.

Now place your hands upon your heart. Feel the beating of your heart. The slow tempo rhythmically beats in tandem with your slow breathing, the essence of your being. Focus here for a moment, feeling the sensation of life within.

Now listen to the thoughts in your mind, which may have been chattering and commenting upon your progress thus far. Step back from the chatter as you would in departing from a conversation with a friend. Wave good-bye, and step into the silent space of your being. Let the chatter move by the space, gently drifting out of your consciousness. Continue to breathe deeply, feeling the vastness of your essence. Focus on your essence as an active way to let go of the chatter. Breathe life, deeply and fully.

Remember this silent place within, this place of quiet nothingness. It may seem empty, but it is alive with your essence.

Connecting with the Angels

We all have guardian angels, divine beings who watch over and guide us through this life. These beings have been with us for many lifetimes, and this bond is close and unique. Working in tandem with your higher spirit-self, angels act as messengers, bringing you ideas and clarity in the darkness. They nudge and move us forward to our destined path, the one we chose with God to walk upon.

Jesus worked closely with his angelic guides to tap into the wisdom and grace of his being. During his youth, Jesus would get flashes of inspiration and great ideas about the complex workings of life. He would feel a great knowingness about a subject, even though he may not have studied it yet. Like Jesus in his childhood, you may have encountered the loving energy of your angels but were unaware of the source of this inspiration. Always by your side, these divine beings gently steer you into situations that will awaken you to your true potential. Reconnecting with your angelic guides will feel like meeting old, dear friends again.

Metatron

As a commanding angel over all legions of angels, Metatron oversees all divine functions performed by angels. He provides tremendous energy for use in manifesting change at the energetic level. When a situation is stuck, Metatron is called in to physically and energetically get it moving. When help is needed in an urgent situation on Earth, Metatron provides energy to heal and change the course of the incident. He is empowered by God and by the infinite source of energy for the universe to act on behalf of the request of the higher spirit-self for assistance.

Metatron can help you to access your divine power when you feel confused, scared, or lost. You can tap into his energy to manifest a solution and change the course of your life. He can help you to heal physical ailments by providing an energetic means to mend your body. His incredible power is available to change your life path and help you to connect with the divine.

This powerful angel works in concert with all angels, saints, ascended masters, and directly with beings on Earth. Let his energy, this life force divine, be your own. Often in our closed-off world, we expend our seemingly limited supply of energy. We spin our wheels, huff and puff up the hill, and feel like we are wasting our time and energy. Metatron reminds us that our energy is not limited when we open ourselves to the divine source of energy. Opening the chakras and reestablishing our divine connection with the higher spirit-self puts us back in touch with our own personal divine power for manifesting peace, love, and joy in our lives.

Connect with the unlimited power source of God through the following visualization.

Divine Power Visualization

Close your eyes, taking a moment to breathe deeply. Let the air cleanse your mind, spirit, and body as you inhale, and allow all old fear-based energies to leave your being as you exhale. When you feel light and clear of blocking energies, open your crown chakra by visualizing the top of the purple ball opening to the heavens, flipping back like the lid on a hinged box.

Now call upon Metatron by saying, *Metatron, be with me now and restore my divine power.*

See a large white stream of energy enter your crown chakra. Feel it as it courses through your body, filling it completely. This intense energy then enters your base chakra, the red ball at the base of your spine. Suddenly it shoots up through the rest of your chakras: orange, yellow, green, blue, indigo, and purple. It bursts out of your head and streams directly upward to the divine source of all energy. As the white stream of energy connects into this divine source, an electric force courses through your body, linking you forevermore with your divine power.

Slowly close your crown chakra. Notice how the energy still streams through the chakra even though it is closed. The energy, still entering your body, quickly fills the four energy fields around your body. Pulsing white energy shines and flashes brilliantly around you, and you watch as it turns a majestic royal purple. You feel comforted, warm, and completely full of divine power and energy.

Open your eyes knowing that you have connected into your divine power and the source of all love.

Archangel Uriel

To know ourselves is divine. To truly understand ourselves and how we have shaped our world is one way to gracefully release old energy and link back into our higher spirit-self. Archangel Uriel, a divine counselor who heals emotional and mental pain, worked directly with Jesus to help him to understand and release old behavior patterns. She is available to you to provide clarity on your life issues. The human mind is inquisitive, and we have a strong desire to know how things work. By understanding our behavior, we are able to grow and change, leaving behind old patterns that do not serve us well.

Uriel would come to Jesus during his dreams to work through complex issues that he felt would hinder him in leading others as the Messiah. Jesus grew up in a male-dominated patriarchal society that used brutality and the fear of scarcity as a way to teach children how to behave in the world. While Mary and Joseph tried to protect Jesus and his siblings from the harsher aspects of this life, he saw how these methods could scar the psyches of the children and adults around him. As a natural course of existing in this environment, Jesus was affected by the conventional methods of interaction among the Israelites. He felt that he needed to release these patterns from his own being before he could teach others how to live in peace.

Uriel would use metaphoric dreams to show Jesus how his earthly life had defined his being, helping him to release patterns that did not serve him or others. Jesus faced a challenge as a Messiah of peace: he had to embody peace even though he was asking others to buck conventional teachings and the authority of the day. Speaking against the Romans, the temple authorities, and religious leaders was seen as an act of treason. But Jesus was asking people to follow the heart of God within, rather than looking outside of themselves for the authority to live spiritual lives. He was calling for peace among all people and an end to the religious caste system. These calls for peace in a savage world were met with ridicule and fear because peace meant changing the core beliefs of a hostile society. Jesus needed help from Uriel to truly be prepared to do that task.

One night as Jesus was sleeping, he slipped into a deep dream state. Uriel began to weave an intricate dream that would illustrate the task ahead and the lessons to learn. Jesus dreamed that he was walking beside a river. In the river, he could see men floating by on their backs, waving their swords in the air. They did not pay attention to the path of their swords, so other men were being stabbed and decapitated in the melee.

Jesus waded out into the river, but he too was cut by the blades. Suddenly, a burst of white light surrounded Jesus, lifting him above the watery carnage. He held his hands over the men in the water, dissolving their swords. The men seemed to awaken from their watery journey and stand up in the river. They looked around in bewilderment, searching for their swords. Jesus bathed them in white light, restoring their battered bodies. For a moment, the men looked at each other and embraced as brothers. Then Jesus began to rise to the heavens. Looking down, he could see embraces turning into shoves and hands turning into knives. The bloodied water continued to flow down the river.

When you need clarity and understanding about your current path and your divine path, turn to Uriel. Use the following affirmation before bed to ask for divine guidance during your dreams.

Divine Dream Affirmation

> I am a great being of light and love.
> I hold the universe within my essence.
> Within my core, I hold unlimited knowledge and
>   understanding.
> Tonight, I ask for that inner knowing to be revealed to me.
> I trust in my divine protector to gently guide me to peace.
> I trust that all I need is within me.

Ariel

Jesus looked to the divine for information on when and how he should approach people with his teachings. The divine helped him every step of the way, leading him along the most fruitful path. Ariel provided Jesus with the knowledge of the past, present, and future of his journey. She gave him a roadmap with instructions for who he should choose as his disciples, temples he should teach outside of, men who would be sympathetic to his cause and those who would not, and friends who would help him along the journey. She provided the structure for his work as the Messiah among the people.

God did not ask Jesus to take on this enormous task on his own. Legions of angels and masters worked together to create the coming of Christ. As the divine incarnate, Jesus had at his disposal many angels to help him with specific actions. Ariel specifically designed his journey to have the maximum effect upon that ancient society and our world today. Revealing the heart of God and the inner workings of the divine realm is an important step in the evolution of the world. Jesus gladly linked with the divine for guidance on executing this master plan.

Hear now as Ariel explains how every person has a divine plan and the ability to access this blueprint for existence:

Dear ones, you have carefully charted your path on Earth, maximizing opportunities to learn new things and resolve old issues with your soul family. Nothing is left to chance on your journey. Your higher spirit-self knows the divine goals of your time here and is gently moving you to achieve these objectives. Just as Jesus linked in with angelic guides to receive guidance and input on his actions, you too can connect with your higher spirit-self and other divine beings for information. You are a vast, multidimensional being, spread between realms of existence. Open your link and life becomes a sweet exploration of the unlimited essence within your being.

You are not alone on this journey, and many angelic beings are ready and willing to help you on your chosen path. Use the following meditation to receive divine guidance for your life.

Divine Guidance Meditation

Find a quiet spot to sit comfortably. You may wish to have paper and a pen close by to write down the divine guidance you will receive. Arrange your body into a position of welcoming acceptance of the divine information you will receive. Close your eyes and breathe deeply. After a few moments, say, *I willingly release all blocks and fears to hearing divine guidance.*

See a brilliant white light surround your body. In a flash, it moves through your being, pulling out all old energy. The light is then sucked up into the space above, disappearing with your old energy. Now see a golden pink light envelop your being, filling you with peace and love.

Now ask that Jesus be with you as you ask for divine guidance by saying, *Jesus, be with me now as I connect with my divine team for guidance.*

See Jesus by your side. Look around Jesus and notice the members of your divine team. Relax and allow the visions to come through. If you do not see the members, feel in your heart who is next to Jesus. Take a moment and allow these impressions to come through.

Now ask your divine team to give you guidance on your path. Allow the images, words, thoughts, or feelings to flow into your being. You may take notes as the information flows into you if you so desire. Let your team have a moment to give you this guidance.

When the message is complete, take a moment to think of any questions you have for your team. You may wish to know their names, who they are in the divine realm, or you may have specific questions about your life issues. Write down your questions or mentally ask them of your team. Again, relax and allow the information to flow through.

When the messages are complete, open your eyes knowing that you are linked with the wisdom of the divine.

Connect frequently with your divine team, knowing that

you are a brave, wonderful being who is on the path to your own personal transformation.

Connecting with the Infinite Source

Just like Jesus, you have many divine beings helping you on your journey. No journey is judged as large or small, for we all are God's children, and we all have unique gifts to offer to humanity. When you connect with the divine, you link into the infinite source of your being. This source hums with the energy of a million experiences, all created by divine beings having a human experience on Earth.

Connecting with saints, masters, and angels takes courage and faith. It takes the ability to set aside doubt and to trust that God will share the details of our divine plan with us. It takes hope and belief that all is well and in order in the universe, and that this type of open communion with the unseen world of Spirit is as natural as talking with your neighbor. It takes an open mind and a willingness to remember all of the great resources available for God's creations to use. And finally, it takes great joy to step back into the world of our beloved divine friends, feeling for a moment the happiness and peace of our eternal self.

Jesus found that the more he connected with his divine team, the more he experienced the joy of living. He had an enormous task to do, but he proceeded with great joy and knowingness that he was doing God's will and his own. There is freedom in moving unrestricted through a restricted world, graced by the power of Spirit.

One day after meeting with a group of people outside of a temple, Jesus felt restless. He was bursting with divine power, and he felt that he needed to share his joy with others. He found his friends cooking a meal when he came calling upon them.

"Come, sit with us, dear Jesus," they said when they saw him approaching the courtyard.

Greeting them all with warm hugs and kisses upon their cheeks, Jesus sat down at a low outdoor table. Smiling, Jesus felt the uncontainable energy within him burst forth and envelop his friends. Suddenly, all conversation stopped and the friends turned to look at each other. Laughter rang out among the group.

"It is great to be alive," Jesus said, hugging the friends on either side of him.

7

Step Five:
Discovering Your Higher Purpose

JESUS found early on in his journey that he had a higher purpose in being born during ancient times of conflict between the Romans and the Jews. Romans occupied not only Israel, but also the holiest of Jewish temples in Jerusalem, limiting the Jews' freedom to live and practice their religion. Jews looked outside of themselves to Jewish temple authorities and Roman government leaders for guidance on how to live honorably, in civic as well as religious duties. Romans governed commerce activities, while Jewish leaders oversaw all religious aspects of life, which extended to the smallest of details to maintain the laws of purity. The life and choices of Jews were not driven by their own inner wisdom but instead dictated by the outer conventional rules of Jewish and Roman society. Jesus' higher purpose was to challenge this outward focus, and show Jews how to shift to an inward focus on the wisdom of the divine self, and allow the laws of God to authentically govern their daily interactions.

Jesus experienced very quickly the challenge of going against the outer-focused conventional religious teachings of the time. In that early religious caste system, temple leaders held power and wealth over most of the Jewish population. These leaders were Jews themselves, but they wielded the same type of authority as the Romans over the poor and middle-class Jews. They had a distinct advantage over most of society, collecting tithes as the middlemen to God. Giving money to the temple was seen as a part of worshiping God. In a sense, the common people paid the religious leaders to have a relationship with God for them inside the inner realms of the temple, where it was believed that the presence of God graced the Earth. The common people were seen as unclean and unworthy to enter these inner rooms of the temple or feel the presence of God. Many of these people were even denied access to the outer rooms of the temple to pray.

Jesus found that preaching outside of the established and respected system meant that he would be labeled a heretic, blasphemer, and traitor to the people of Israel and the Roman empire. And yet he had to believe in his own power as an inspired leader of the people, whether or not others legitimized his actions by their belief in his words. He had to trust that his divine purpose was more important than acceptance into religious and conventional society. He had to shift from an outward focus of acceptance by others to an inward focus of commitment to the strong connection he felt with God, and the need to convey this very real communion as a way of life for all.

We too have experienced the pain of looking to others to validate our choices and behavior in society. Finding your divine purpose requires a shift in your belief system from pleasing others to serving the God of your heart. Service to God is not always the popular choice in society, and you have to be willing to let go of your fears of not being accepted by others because you have chosen this path. But ultimately, this choice is not so foreign because others, such as Jesus and the saints and masters before and after him, have opened the gate for us to walk upon our intended divine path of purpose.

Jesus experienced this change from an outward to an inward focus through his experiences with the people of Israel, as well as through his own inner work. His angel came to him one afternoon while he was meditating alone in the wilderness. Sitting comfortably under a tree, Jesus could see his angel floating toward him. He smiled and greeted her.

Sitting down beside Jesus, the angel said, "Dear Jesus, you are ready to know the secret purpose of your higher spirit-self."

Jesus looked at her and creased his eyebrows in confusion. "Why is it a secret?"

"For you have not known it, not truly felt the power of your higher spirit-self. You know that you will represent the essence of God, and be the human representative of the divine. But there is more to it than that, and until this moment it has not been revealed to you and others on Earth," said the angel, smiling.

Jesus leaned forward and eagerly said, "Tell me more, dear angel."

The angel moved in front of Jesus and placed her forehead against his.

"I will show you."

Images began to flood his mind's eye, and Jesus could see into the future, the present, and the past simultaneously. It was as if every moment moved together in harmony, all actions were one action, and all participants were the same. The angel sat back and looked expectantly at Jesus.

"Now, master, you tell me what you see and what the secret is," she said softly.

Jesus, still in the moment of the simultaneous, could see all events merging as one. Over and over again, like waves churning upon the shore, moments occurred in the past, present, and future. He could see his birth moment merging with the births of all other prophets, and in that instant he knew that he carried the energy and momentum of all who walked this path before him. All events were one and the same in that they were connected in importance and the necessity to occur. All roads led to this moment and all others like it.

Jesus looked up at his angel and said, "The secret is that there is no secret. All of the past pointed to this moment, as all of my actions will point to another moment. We are all connected by the power of energy and the choices we make in the moment."

The angel smiled. "You, my friend, have connected into the true power of your mastery."

Understanding Your Divine Plan

Like Jesus, we are moving forward in the momentum created by the never-ending cycle of human life on Earth. Our triumphs of great scientific and intellectual discoveries about our world, as well as our failures of perpetual wars of conflict, shape our experience of life and how we choose to move forward. Choices made by ancestors in the past affect future generations. We can move like wheels on an old covered wagon, traveling the same rutted roads of the past, well worn and accepted by others. Or we can forge new paths, basing our desired outcomes on the higher ideals and principles set forth by our divine plan.

A divine plan represents what you would ideally like to achieve during your life. Your job is to remember this mission by reconnecting with the original drafters of the plan: God and your higher spirit-self. Divine plans vary widely but hold a common thread: reconnect with Spirit and end the feeling of separation from God. Beyond that great task, your plan may include experiencing situations that will teach you more about yourself, helping others in a certain capacity, making amends with others, inspiring others, or honoring God.

During your life's journey, you discover new and familiar experiences, and through these events, you learn more about yourself. You have made a plan with God and your higher spirit-self about what you will explore in this life. You may need to resolve old issues that have stayed with you from other life experiences, such as betrayal, judgment, murder, victimization, and other challenges. In Eastern traditions, these energies are known as karmic experiences, which you need to resolve with others. Many of us come to Earth multiple times with the same soul group, which consists of our family and friends. We may play the same familial role again, or switch places within the soul group in order to resolve and release old karmic issues. Releasing old karmic energy allows you to access dharmic energy, which Eastern traditions define as experiences that have propelled you closer to enlightenment during your many lifetimes. Dharmic energy includes compassion, love, faith, wisdom, and other like energies that move you to greater levels of understanding, which expands your breadth of service to God and humanity.

When you tap into your divine plan, life loses its uncertainty.

Jesus knew that his acceptance of the outcasts of society would put him in conflict with the wealthy, the religious authorities, and the Romans. But those associations were a part of his divine mission from God, so he willingly cultivated these relationships in order to teach others directly how to embody and live within the Spirit of God in daily life. Jesus followed his heart, meaning he linked directly with Spirit for guidance and direction in pursuing his divine mission.

Your life path becomes clear when you begin to move forward in concert with the divine. But many of us fear the unknown of the future, and we develop control and power issues as a symptom of that fear. We become afraid to take risks or try something new outside of our realm of control. But this type of control actually keeps us in a state of paralysis, very much out of control. In this frozen state, the very things that we fear can happen, rocking our world and our foundation of existence. Our fears become energized by our focus on controlling them, so they become manifest in our world.

The first step to real control is releasing our stronghold of fear. In acknowledging and releasing the fear, we can then allow authentic control to enter our lives. Authentic control is direct access to your divine plan and the means to carry it forth. Knowing your mission in coming to Earth now and how to accomplish it frees you from the fear of the unknown. For most people, knowing your divine purpose does not mean that you will see into the future and control every action related to your path. Knowing your mission means that you understand the direction you are moving in, and you become open and ready to capitalize on moments that will propel you forward. You become a willing player in the symphony of divine movement in our world, because you become open to achieving your divine purpose. You walk without fear, and instead move forward with the hope of finding a new spark to light your internal flame of knowledge in that moment. You become a divine being actualizing a divine plan through a human experience on Earth.

How can you find out your divine purpose?

Jesus found out his mission after he began releasing old energy of fear, pain, anger, disillusionment, rejection, judgment, and the effects of scarcity from his being. As you let go of these illusions of life, you open yourself to divine guidance. Letting go of the old allows you to access the new in your life. Part of the human growth process is releasing, reconnecting, and remembering our inner heart through exploring and performing our divine plan. Know that you possess the ability within you to access the divine and that each step you take will lead you to that place of understanding your divine purpose.

What is needed to remember your divine purpose?

We often see Jesus as a superhuman role model because of his ability to heal the sick and lead others back to their inner hearts.

We may worry that we need those abilities to realize our divine plan. To remember your divine purpose, you just need to hold a strong will and intention to let go of old energy that blocks your divine connection and become conscious of the choices you make in life. You need not hold a belief in religion, God, Jesus, angels, ascended masters, saints, eternal life, or even miracles to begin this journey. You only need to hold a conviction in your heart that you desire to let go of the illusions of life and tap into your own personal stream of wisdom. There are many roads to enlightenment, and another being cannot presume to tell you how to go through your release process. But you are never alone upon your journey. You have access to divine beings who will guide and assist you in a way that honors your path and helps you to achieve the goals of your divine plan.

Jesus wanted to know his divine plan in great detail to assuage his fears of leading others. In his divine contract with God, Jesus agreed to embrace the poor, the sick, and all other outcasts as a way to awaken society to the ills and pain of a life of separation from God. The culmination of his earthly contract with God was enduring an early, public death so that others might remember the way to eternal life. His role was clearly revealed to him by his divine team, and he willingly explored and performed this divine work because it was a part of his divine plan. Some may wonder how Jesus could embrace death, but he knew that it was an important part of his mission. He knew that the road he was to walk would be bumpy, but he also knew that he was not alone. God and his divine team would support him every step of the way with loving compassion, giving him the strength needed to perform his divine role.

"Lord, I am just a simple carpenter's son," Jesus said to God one day during meditation. "I do not know that I can perform the tasks that you ask of me."

At that moment, Jesus felt a warmth in his belly, and it slowly spread throughout his entire body, filling his being. He felt like a butterfly in a chrysalis, enfolded in a nurturing environment of love and peace. Through the darkness, he could make out shapes around him, but he could not see any light. Layers of darkness began to lift from his form, and he slowly could see a bright, brilliant world around him.

He wasn't afraid any longer.

"Lord, my father in heaven, I would follow you to the ends of the Earth to do your bidding," Jesus whispered, tears running down his cheeks. "Let me know this peace always."

"I need not let you know anything, dear Jesus," God gently replied to his inner ears. "You already possess this peace within. I only open your eyes to the heart of God within you. Blessed be you, my son, my creation of love and understanding. Know this and know this only: I am within you and you never hold reason to be afraid on this journey of the heart."

Explorers and Performers in the New World

Like Jesus did, you can remember your higher purpose in living on Earth at this time. You can tap into your divine plan in two ways: as an explorer or as a performer. At times you may experience a personal journey of divine exploration, while in other moments you may perform a specific divine function that is visible to others. The choice to explore or perform in any given moment is up to you.

Hear now as God explains actualizing your divine purpose:

Dear ones, when you set out for Earth, you decide in great detail what you would like to achieve. You work closely with me and others in the divine realm to determine how you might serve humanity, as well as moving forward my divine plan for life on Earth. You create a plan of purpose, and when you begin the path of spiritual awakening on Earth, you may choose to actualize your plan as an explorer or a performer.

If you choose to explore, you will realize your divine plan on the personal level, learning more about yourself and your circle of friends and family. You gain rich experiences and great knowledge about yourself in a world overshadowed by fear and feelings of separation from God.

If you choose to perform, you become an agent of change for God. You take your divine plan and actualize it in the outer world, affecting others beyond your circle through your words, actions, and deeds. You become a reminder to others that they too must awaken and begin to realize their divine plan.

As you can see by my words, you can both explore and perform your divine plan. You may do both at different times in your life and on many different levels. You may explore overcoming pain by leaving an abusive relationship. Later, you may perform your divine plan by counseling other people on how to let go of the pain of these types of relationships. We can only teach what we ourselves have experienced. As you know with life, you are always learning and growing, and one of the great things about tapping into your divine purpose is the great joy of discovering more about yourself on all levels.

Jesus' divine purpose was to bridge the gap between heaven and Earth and remind humanity of their inner connection with the divine. During his journey, he explored the depths of his being, as well as performing specific actions that were a part of God's plan for bringing peace to Earth. Upon his awakening, he was told and shown in many ways what his function required him to do. He willingly and knowingly chose to enter into service with the divine in order to explore and perform his divine function here on Earth.

Jesus learned more about his divine role as he cleared out old energy and invited more of the loving knowledge of the divine to become a part of his daily life. As he dipped more into this divine knowledge stream, he was able to claim the wisdom of his higher spirit-self and access it from his human form. Jesus may have felt fear at times during his role as the Messiah, but he could always release that pain and connect with a greater understanding of the universe and his role in that moment of time. His personal exploration into the inner realms of his being aided him in performing his divine function and in modeling the choice of letting the divine self touch others upon Earth.

As Jesus began his ministry, he connected with many different people. Some were immediately moved to join him, while others felt threatened by his radical teachings. Others liked his message and supported his teachings from afar but did not directly join his group. Jesus knew that all of these responses from people he met were valid: the choice to remain asleep, explore, or perform would help each individual learn more about himself or herself and become an example for future generations. Jesus knew that his mark upon the Earth would be far-reaching and would not end with his physical death.

As he began teaching outside of temples, his talks drew large crowds. Many of the people who came to hear him speak were poor and clung to the lower rungs of society. These outcasts were shunned by society, but to Jesus they represented a part within all of us that we wish to hide. Humans wish to cloak their frailty and failures to present their best side to others. These people, through their own circumstances and those created by society, could not hide their lowly existence. They possessed none of the trappings of the wealthy to hold in front of themselves to appear as anything more than poor. They existed on the basest level of survival, and in their desperation, they were willing to try something new to improve their life situations. These were the people who were most likely to embrace Jesus, for he represented a way to a new life where they could be accepted and not shunned from society.

Among the crowds, Jesus would focus on the most downhearted and downtrodden of people, who were often women. He embraced all people, rich and poor, but he found that his message of finding the God within shook people up the most when applied to the outcasts of society. Many Israelites were willing to accept the holiness of religious leaders, but they did not extend that willingness to the underbelly of society.

One day outside of a temple, Jesus was approached by a small group of women who heard that this master would allow women to hear his teachings. Standing near him, they spoke to him indirectly so as not to draw attention to themselves.

"I hear that this teacher Jesus allows women to learn from him," said one of the women to her friends.

Jesus, sitting behind them, said, "It is true that I openly welcome women to hear my message and be moved by my words."

Still not looking at him, the woman continued, "I hear that Jesus teaches that husbands should respect their wives as the wife respects the husband."

Again, Jesus answered, "It is true that I ask husbands not to falsely accuse their wives of injustices that they themselves commit. I only ask that husbands treat their wives as objects of respect and not as objects of property."

"Then it is true," the woman said to her friends, "that this Jesus is different from other teachers. I know not whether to believe his sincerity in protecting the rights of women, or whether he covets the women for himself."

Jesus laughed loudly, making the women jump. "It is true that I covet women, but only as a brother would hold concern for a sister. Your honor is safe with me, for I honor that we both were created by God. This bond holds us to honor and respect each other, not dominate or put in servitude one of God's creations."

Looking up toward the temple gates, the woman noticed a temple official eyeing the group. Pushing the other women to go, she turned away from the official and said to Jesus under her breath, "You may honor me, but the others do not."

As the women left, Jesus closed his eyes in prayer.

Using the Christ Model to Discover Your Purpose

Discovering your divine purpose is a natural part of a spiritual awakening. As you release old energy, your true essence begins to shine through, and you naturally begin to move in a guided direction to realize your divine plan. To hasten this process, you can use the Christ model of purpose as a guide to remembering your divine purpose.

The Christ model of purpose is threefold:

1. Let go of the pain in your life.
2. Allow the divine to guide your way.
3. Act upon divine guidance to help yourself and others upon the path.

Simplified even further, the model becomes: release, listen, and act.

This model is simple because your divine purpose is encoded in your being, awaiting activation by your conscious reconnection with Spirit. Discovering your divine plan is just like the process of remembering your shopping list in your head when you go to the grocery store. As you see fruit in the bin, bread on the shelf, and cheese in the refrigerator, your memory is jogged, and you pick up that item and put it in your cart. When you do conscious release work of old blocking energy, the events and experiences of your life jog your memory, and you hold them up for inspection. You get a nagging feeling that you are forgetting something important, something that you know you wanted to do. Inspiration comes to you through meditation, during a walk in nature, or while in conversation with a friend. God's messages come to us in many forms, and just by being open to remembering your divine purpose, it will come to you. Be ready and willing to release, listen, and act.

Just like Jesus, we begin our journey as explorers, looking deeply at our life experiences and then letting them go. As explorers, we recognize that we cannot serve others without serving the self first. You, as a human being, become the first recipient of God's love and grace in your world. Allow that grace to release old pain and illusions in your life. In ministering to yourself first, you become an open vessel for the divine to work through you. Saint Francis prayed to God to make him an instrument, to use him to perform his divine work. To be an instrument of God, a performer of your divine plan, you need to drop all pretenses that keep you separate from your creator source and allow that inspiration to flow through you.

Hear now God's words to help you to follow the Christ model of purpose:

My dear ones, just as Jesus reached out to many other beings in pain, you too can reach out to a person in pain: yourself.

Look within first before looking outside to others. Clear your home of the old before inviting others in. When you have cleared old energy blocking you from your higher spirit-self, you may then listen to that still voice within for guidance on your purpose. Quiet, still, silent—allow the divine to touch you and help lead you to your chosen path. Take a moment to let your path come to the light of day, and let it touch your heart, for this is an exquisite moment of revelation. Now act upon divine guidance for realizing your purpose in this world. We are all here to serve in some capacity, and you will feel great joy in letting your heart open to help others. Serve the self first, then serve others as the true divine being you are.

Just as Jesus learned to see the God within others, you too can see the light of divinity dwelling within all beings. Following the path of Jesus' awakening, you can find your purpose in this world. Jesus did his own inner work to become the man of peace that God asked him to be. He knew that to serve others with a full, open heart, he had to free himself from his own pain. This freedom allowed him to see others in the light of compassion, love, and acceptance, no matter what the situation. Each experience he encountered gave him the chance to choose love, in himself and in others.

It was no different that day as he walked through the public square. He could see a commotion up ahead: a fallen woman surrounded by an angry crowd.

"Speak to me now, oh God, for I do not know what I have done wrong," the woman cried as she lay broken upon the ground. A prostitute, shunned from society, hurt and shamed by her fellow humans, she felt no hope that God would ever allow her into the kingdom of heaven.

Reaching the edge of the crowd, Jesus looked upon the woman with compassion while others shunned her.

"She is evil, one of the demons from hell," people said of her. And yet men would take of her flesh without a thought to her origins or the inner hell that tormented her while taking part in these acts for a few pieces of gold or food to eat.

Now she lay in the dirt, alone and unwanted, used one too many times. Jesus moved forward and stood beside her. Kneeling down, he helped her to sit up while people looked on at them in horror.

"He touched her," the crowd murmured. "He too wants to partake of her sin."

Ignoring the buzzing anger around him, Jesus spoke to the young woman with a tenderness she had never known before.

"My child, you too are a daughter of God," he said softly.

People nearby were immediately outraged by this statement and repeated it to others in the crowd with disbelief.

As if they were the only people in the public square, Jesus continued to minister to the woman.

"My child, I feel the pain in your heart and know that you only act to put food on your table. And yet I say to you, within your heart, you hold the grace of an angel of God. Let go of these actions and find a way to honor yourself and the God that dwells within you," Jesus said softly to the crying woman.

"I am nothing in this world," she said, sobs wrenching her

small frame. "I do not know where to go from here."

"Go inside, into your father's house. The house of the Lord dwells within us all," Jesus replied. "I say to you, your sins are forgiven. Go forth, walking the path of the Lord, serving others as God serves and honors you."

The crowd was shouting, cursing Jesus and the woman.

Helping the woman to her feet, Jesus placed an arm around her shoulders and raised his other hand to silence the crowd. An angry hush fell among the people.

"I say to you all, let he among you without sin cast the first stone upon this woman," Jesus said.

Men looked at neighbors who had wronged them; beggars, who relied on the charity of others, turned their eyes downward; and tax collectors took a step back from the crowd.

Raising his hands over the crowd, Jesus said, "Your sins are no greater or smaller than the sins of this woman. But she alone holds something that you do not. She holds the desire to let God wash her of her sins, take away the pain within her, and restore her anew. She asked God today to do this for her, and I say to her today that her sins are forgiven. I say to you today that your sins are forgiven, but will you let that change your world? Today, this woman let it change her world."

As the crowd slowly dispersed, the woman turned to Jesus, smiling through her tears. "I will not disappoint you, Lord. I will do your bidding to change."

Holding her hands in his, Jesus replied, "I do not ask anything of you, dear child. Listen to your heart to know God's will for you, and in doing so, you honor me."

Simple Path of Purpose

Simplicity is the key to accessing the wisdom and purpose of your higher spirit-self and integrating these qualities into daily life. Remember how simple things seemed during childhood? A new child in the neighborhood could just walk over and ask to play with you. You accepted this child into your world because he lived right next door. That proximity of life forged an instant rapport and need within both of you: treat this child as a member of my family because we live close and play together. As you grew older, a new awareness of your body, burgeoning sexual desires, and a need to fit in with the right group crowded out your simple need to treat your neighbor with love and respect. Life no longer held simplicity, so you adopted other ways to deal with your anxieties and worries about fitting in with adult society.

These complexities of life shield us from our divine purpose. You can remember the simple days of childhood. Held within these memories is your divine purpose. That child, that small innocent being, was much closer then to knowing what life is really about now. Remember your unguarded self, and you remember who you are and why you are here.

Hear now the words of Jesus on remembering simplicity in our daily world:

> I say to you, dear ones of the new millennium, I see the yearning within you for a simpler time in your life. Not to idealize the days of youth, but then you held fewer veils, fewer mechanisms for deception to keep others far enough

away so that you would not get hurt. You dance elaborately
with words, thoughts, and emotions to survive in this world.
You are complex and oftentimes hard to understand, by yourself and others. I say to you, dear ones of the heart, I see deep
within you a simpler you. You, who desires peace. You, who
cares for your neighbor. You, who loves to laugh and pretend.
You, a very special you, a simple person with simple needs:
love me for who I am and I will love you for who you are.
Embrace that simple you within.

Holding that simple you within changes how you perceive the
world around you. Discarding layers of pretense, perceived
slights and wrongs, you tap into how Jesus lived his life during
his journey as the Messiah of peace. He was an explorer of the
inner soul, charting unknown territories of the human mind,
spirit, and body. He shared his wisdom as a performer, a living
example of leading a Spirit-driven life to its fullest. But most of
all, he was a tangible piece of the work of God on Earth, a
reminder of the presence of Spirit in our daily world. Tap into
your own peace of heaven by using Jesus' affirmation, his
reminder, for following Spirit in all things to live a life of
purpose.

Heart of God Affirmation

The heart of God dwells within me.
It beats strong in me,
    like never-ending waves upon the shore.

It comforts me,
   like a rainbow promise of life eternal after the storm.
It beckons to me,
   like an old friend leading me home.
It is me, my most sacred self.

8

Step Six:
Moving as a Master
through Your World

THROUGHOUT his journey, Jesus worked on many levels to reclaim his inner mastery. We all hold this inner mastery. It is a part of our divine heritage, an inherent part of our divinity. Our higher spirit-self, who resides simultaneously in a higher level of consciousness, represents our master self, a being of great abundance who feels no separation from God. As you release old pain blocking this awareness of your higher spirit-self, you begin to allow mastery qualities to shine through and govern your daily interactions with others. Faith, compassion, power, wisdom, love, and many other mastery qualities can be expressed on a higher level in your life when you allow your state of mastery to actualize in the present, physical world.

Mastery can be defined in many ways, but in the divine sense, mastery is a conscious state of living in an unconscious environment. Our world frequently operates on autopilot, and we can do many things without thought or regard to the outcome of our actions. In a state of mastery, we shake off the sandman dust coating our thoughts, feelings, emotions, and behavior. We consciously choose to operate on manual pilot, aware of every choice we make in every experience.

Jesus experienced this conscious mastery over and over again as he used the remembrance mastery plan, which is a four-step method for handling life experiences by recognizing the experience, opportunity, choice, and reconnection offered in every situation. He reached a point where life became just a series of experiences, or lessons, that he capitalized upon to reach a greater depth of connection with Spirit. Fear lost its dominant hold over his experiences when he looked for the growth opportunity offered in every moment. His life experiences could no longer knock him down with doubt or frustration. Instead, he took a moment to look at the situation using the remembrance mastery plan, allowing these four steps to awaken his conscious awareness. Even during the painful experiences of trials before Jewish and Roman leaders, Jesus consciously chose to maintain his faith and connection with God. We all have conscious choices and opportunities for reconnection to our inner mastery in the easiest and most difficult experiences.

The remembrance mastery plan reminds us that life is about experience, and each situation is an opportunity to choose greater reconnection with God. Experience, opportunity, choice, and reconnection are reminders that can be used in any situation as a tool for remembering our task as human beings on

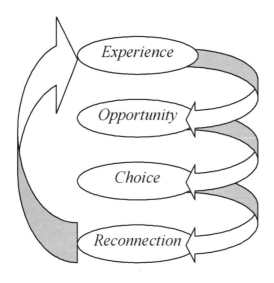

Remembrance Mastery Plan

God's Earth. Every moment is a moment of remembrance of our inherent divinity and mastery.

Experience

Every day you wake up with a plan for the day. You may plan on going to a matinee to see a movie that you have been very excited about, but the phone rings. It's a friend with no close family in the area, who is down with the flu and needs you to bring chicken soup and words of comfort for the afternoon. You may have a moment of wrestling within yourself: movie/friend, friend/movie. You may ask yourself why you have to play nursemaid today when you really just want some time to escape with your celluloid heroes. You may feel angry with your friend for asking you to make this choice when you already have plans for the day. At this point, the outcome of the situation will be determined by your conscious level of decision making.

You have encountered an experience of life. Think about every moment of your day, and you realize that your time has been filled with one experience after another. Some may stick with you while others are forgotten. But one thing remains constant: your life is just one big experience designed to place events in your path that will reawaken you to the heart of God within.

Opportunity

In the movie/friend dilemma, there are many opportunities to remember your inner mastery. You could go to your friend's house with the soup, play Scrabble all afternoon, and end up staying the night. Or you could drop off the soup on your way to the movie. Or you could just go to the movies. With each of these options, you have the opportunity to address issues that have followed you through life. Maybe you have a problem with caring too much for others, and you go overboard in making sure they are fine. This experience could be an opportunity to consider your needs as well as the needs of the other person. For you, dropping off the soup on the way to the matinee would be the masterful thing to do.

Being open to each experience as an opportunity awakens your consciousness to be present in the situation. You may take more time in assessing the situation beyond the initial annoyance it may have caused. You may see an opportunity to address wider issues in your life through this smaller experience of learning.

Choice

After the phone rang, you set down your car keys and listened to your sick friend, recognized that this experience is an opportunity for growth, and now you are ready to make a choice. In making choices in a conscious manner, we take responsibility for our decisions by considering our needs as well as the needs of others. We can make a win-win decision that will benefit both parties involved, even if that means choosing not to help your friend. In contrast, when we unconsciously make choices, it would be easy to say to our sick friend, "Okay, okay, you twisted my arm. I'll forget the movie and come help you." You could grouse about your decision, justifying your anger by saying, "What else could I have done with a sick friend?"

When you access your mastery qualities and make conscious choices, you recognize that others cannot force choices upon you. Only you can make decisions about where you will put your heart and energy.

Reconnection

After your choice is made, the final step in this experience is feeling the outcome of your decision. If you feel good and satisfied with your choice, your mastery energy will flow into you through a greater self-confidence, a greater feeling of love, a sense of accomplishment, or many other feelings that affirm that you are a masterful being. If you feel upset with your choice, it may mean that there will be more experiences coming down the line to help you resolve this issue. Or it may mean that you are on the path to releasing this issue, and you are uncomfortable with trying a new choice rather than being ruled by your old unconscious decisions. Reconnection puts us in touch with our heart of God when we allow our experiences to move us in new directions. When we recognize that we can pull from the greater abundance of our inner wisdom to guide us, we can let go of old painful behaviors in our life. We reconnect with our inner wisdom, which puts us on the path to actualizing our mastery qualities in the present. The more pain you release, the greater the abundance you receive.

In consciously using the four steps of experience, opportunity, choice, and reconnection, you awaken and remember the power you hold within your being. You remember life as greater than what meets the eye. You see beyond the physical world and begin to notice the subtle workings of Spirit in our everyday lives. You become a master of the remembrance mastery plan.

Four Mastery Qualities: Love, Compassion, Forgiveness, and Personal Responsibility

Recognizing the mastery in others allows us to find our own mastery within. Love, compassion, forgiveness, and personal responsibility are four mastery qualities that we all hold. In accessing these qualities, we can move through our world and each experience with grace, honoring ourselves and others. Each of these qualities requires us to reach deeper within ourselves, clearing out old energy that blocks this abundant flow of mastery energy.

Jesus pulled from these abundant qualities within himself when he interacted with the people of ancient Israel. Love guided all of his actions and became the basis of his ministry. Love provides the foundation for our world and is the cornerstone of our existence. When we reach out to others with compassion, we use the power of love to see others in the same light as God sees us. When we forgive ourselves and others, we allow the light of God to change hearts and move forward without pain or regret. When we take personal responsibility for our actions and behavior, we become aware of the power of our choices and the great privilege of being alive in this moment on Earth. When you use all of your God-given mastery qualities of love, compassion, forgiveness, and personal responsibility, you walk with the great masters before you.

Explore each of these mastery qualities now, and access their abundant power to guide your actions in every life experience.

Love of the Master

"Hear me now, oh Father, for I do not know what to do," Jesus prayed one day while outside the city of Jerusalem.

Many people had been following him because he had begun to perform miracles of making more from less. While in front of the people, Jesus called upon his inner strength and wisdom to lead the people as the Messiah. But later when he was alone in meditation, he felt fear about the next steps he would take upon his journey.

He felt a quiet rush of air about him, and he sensed the presence of God within him.

"My son, what troubles you?" God spoke to his inner ears.

"I feel so much from these people. They want and need so much. I can see and feel their pain, and it is immense. Father, how can I fill their needs and help them to let this pain go?" Jesus silently asked.

Suddenly a warm breeze enveloped Jesus. He could feel the wind as if it were a thousand hands, holding, caressing, and loving him. In this moment of the many, Jesus found his answer.

"It is always within me," Jesus said with a quiet laugh. "I show abundance to the people today, and yet I forget that I am made from abundance."

"Yes, dear Jesus," God replied gently. "It is through the grace of many that we are all provided for abundantly. You reminded the people today that my harvest is everlasting, and all they need do is ask and it shall be provided. You, dear Jesus, are bringing my fruits to the people, and you shall receive abundant help in your work."

Just as Jesus discovered, when you reconnect with the divine and begin to understand your divine plan, you connect into an unlimited source of abundance for use in manifesting your divine work. Jesus was not alone in the miracles he performed. He sometimes would worry about his journey, but he would always release that fear and connect back into the source of energy from which all of his works abounded.

The source of this abundance was simple: pure love.

Love is the creative energy that provides all that we know, see, feel, hear, and touch in this world. We are created by love, we are empowered by love, and we are love. God is love, pure and simple, and when we remember this power, this fuel for our being, we tap into our greatest mastery quality.

Love is the basis for all of our actions, great or small. When we awake in the morning, how quickly we jump out of bed is determined by how much love we feel for our task ahead. If we love our job, we skip out of bed. If we feel less than love for our job, we drag ourselves out of bed. If we love our friends, we make time to spend with them. If we feel less than love for our friends, we tell them that we are too busy to get together. Our compassion, forgiveness, and personal responsibility are determined by how much love we feel for ourselves and others in our life. If we feel less than love for ourselves, we demonstrate a lack of love for others. We cannot give to others what we don't feel in our hearts for ourselves.

Hear now as God explains the role of love in a masterful life:

Dear hearts, you are made from love. God loves life and abundance, and the light of my love flows forth from my being, through your heart, and into your physical world. When you let go of old burdens in your life, my light of love shines forth unfettered, glowing brightly and abundantly for all to see. When fear blocks your light, your true essence of love is inhibited, and you feel separate from my love and the love of your higher spirit-self. You begin to doubt, waging war within yourself, and turn away from the source of love you desire. When you turn back to the light, love flows and your world is restored. Fresh, anew, you become an agent of love, touching the hearts of others, reminding them of this tender quality that can move mountains and change the course of the world.

How can you access your mastery quality of love? Look deep within yourself, and know that love already exists below the layers of pain. Love has never left—you only forgot that it was there all along. Turn back to the light of love and it will shine forth, changing your life.

Accessing your inner mastery quality of love is simple. Love is always present. We only need to recognize its presence and allow it to guide our actions. Jesus allowed love to lead his behavior by using a love compass tool, which is a method for aligning your heart with love to more effectively handle any situation. When you shift your focus from fear to love, you can access your divine wisdom more quickly and easily to create solutions that benefit yourself and others. A love compass can guide you through the remembrance mastery plan, aligning your will with God's will and allowing love to be the basis for all of your actions.

The love compass sounds simple because it is a straightforward guide for realizing your divine plan through the power of love.

Love Compass Tool

1. *Experience.* When you are faced with an experience,

state your intention to view it through the lens of love by saying, *I choose to see this experience as an opportunity to let love shine through my being.*

2. *Opportunity.* When reviewing options for a course of action in the experience, ask yourself the following question to determine the amount of love you will need to perform the action: *How much love must I pull from within to perform this action?* The more love you need to act, the greater the connection to Spirit. The less love you need to act, the smaller the connection to Spirit. Accessing more love for every opportunity means that you are pulling from the abundant creative love energy of God.

3. *Choice.* Make your choice based on how much love you will use to perform the action. If you choose the option that requires great love, you are pushing yourself to grow and connect with your inner wisdom for greater power in every experience. You are choosing the life and abundance God holds for every human on Earth. If you choose an action that requires little energy or love on your part, know that you are still working within God's love, but on a lower level. We can reach for greater levels of love in certain situations, maintain current levels of love at other moments, or retreat into a reaction mode of no love at other times. There are no set rules for choosing love. Your intention and will to connect more deeply with God and

your mastery quality of love will set your course in that moment.

4. *Reconnection.* After you have chosen a course of action in the experience, you reconnect with your inner heart to access the power of love to manifest the outcome. You may meditate for guidance on moving ahead, you may visualize a loving outcome using the power of Spirit, or you may use an affirmation to bring forth more love from your being to take action in the situation, such as, *I am love in every moment. I let love guide my way. I see love in you. I unite in love with you.* You also may use the following statement of intention as a way to access love for the outcome, as well as inviting Spirit to work through you as an instrument of love: *I willingly move forward using the power, grace, and love of Spirit to actualize a loving outcome in this experience.*

Compassion of the Master

Just as Jesus knew, reaching out to others despite who they are, where they come from, and what they represent to society, comes from your own inner mastery. A master walks unfettered upon the Earth, not bound by the conventions of others, not fearing what people will think when he reaches out with compassion to others. Compassion is the recognition that the needs of others are not so different from our own needs. The pain of others is not so different from our own pain. That commonality bonds us more than any other external judgment factors we use in our daily lives to separate ourselves from others.

When you can accept yourself and others right where you are, you can access your inner mastery quality of compassion. Compassion is the ability to feel empathy for others and act toward them in a nonjudgmental way. It is based on the belief that we should hold the highest and best thoughts about others in our hearts. On this journey of life, sometimes people fall down and may not be able to find their way. In having compassion, or a belief in the highest and best for others, you become an energy marker for their potential. In other words, you have faith that their ability to be an instrument of God is greater than they are actually demonstrating in this moment. This recognition of their greater potential can be a hidden gift, because compassionate intentions do not need to be known by the recipient for the blessings to flow upon them. Jesus demonstrated this every time he recognized a person as a child of God. He accepted prostitutes, tax collectors, sinners—the very people that conventional wisdom deemed as unworthy of compassion. He believed in them, giving them the power to actualize their greatness.

Jesus found that when he connected with his own mastery, he could see others for who they truly were: human creations of God. That inherent goodness, that inherent divinity, bound him to treat his fellow humans as he himself would desire to be treated: with respect, love, and compassion. Jesus viewed all humans as equal because each one was created with great love and care by God. He felt that it was an act of ignorance to treat other human beings as anything less than vital to life. As a master, he recognized the mastery within others.

You too hold this capability within you to see the mastery within others and to treat them with respect, love, and compassion. In our divine plans, we all hold a common goal: to awake and connect with the divine as a conscious, sentient being. In our old closed worlds of pain, we can see others as our persecutors and ourselves as victims. In reality, we are the same as others in that we desire to feel peace and a sense of belonging. It is this common bond of oneness, this desire for the same thing, that makes us one, made of the same cloth.

Time and time again, in his travels and in his teachings, Jesus demonstrated this unity of being we all hold in this shared experience of human life.

"Over here," the Roman soldier said, as he showed Jesus a man lying upon the ground.

Jesus traveled far and wide through the countryside, and the inhabitants of the land did not influence his choice of roads. As he knelt beside a middle-aged Gentile man, some of Jesus' followers could not believe that he would touch this unholy flesh.

"Get this man a drink of water," Jesus said to one of his followers.

Doubtfully, a follower took some water from his pack and gave it to the man to drink.

"Help him to sit up," Jesus told another disciple.

With a look of disgust, the disciple helped the man into a sitting position, but he was too weak to remain upright on his own. Giving Jesus a questioning look, the disciple began to lay the man back down.

"Give him your own back to lean against," Jesus said.

With a groan, the disciple again helped the man to sit up and then quickly moved behind him so that he could support the man's weight.

"Wash his feet," Jesus told another disciple. With that statement, all of the disciples protested that they would not bow down to a non-Jewish peasant in this subservient way.

"Then I shall do it for you," Jesus said, pulling out water and oil from his own satchel.

"Master, no," said one disciple. "Let me."

"Why do you beg to do this now?" Jesus asked. "No, the honor is mine, and I take it for my own."

Gently, Jesus poured water on the man's feet, using his own clothes to wipe the man's feet clean. Then he gently applied oil upon the withered flesh. The man looked at Jesus, tears rolling down his cheeks.

"No one has ever done that for me," he whispered. "I know who you are. Please, take this pain from me."

An angry murmur arose among the disciples.

"I can only take away that which you do not want. Do you believe in everlasting life?" Jesus asked the man.

The man wrinkled his brow in confusion. "I wish to keep life eternal but not this pain."

Jesus smiled. "Then it is done."

Placing his hands upon the man's head, a great hush fell

among the group. The man began rocking back and forth, moaning. Suddenly, he stood up of his own will.

"The pain is gone," he yelled, embracing Jesus.

Just like Jesus, you can release old, threatening ideas about others you encounter on your path. Jesus learned through experience, opportunity, choice, and reconnection how to access his inner compassion. He consciously chose to be compassionate in his encounters with others. He also learned how to be compassionate by observing others demonstrate this mastery quality.

During his time on Earth, Jesus was touched by the compassion of his mother, Mary. She accepted him completely as the Messiah when others did not. She accepted the experiences that occurred during Jesus' rise as the Messiah, as well as the end of his days as a man of peace on Earth. Mary honored in Jesus the very thing that he honored in her.

We too can access our mastery quality of compassion and honor others in our life. We become selective of the people we accept in our lives, and if they seem different or foreign, we often reject them. But in accepting the new in your life, you are able to let go of the old preconceptions about the world and learn how to see the goodness in all beings. We are all made of the same divine cloth, gently cut out and lovingly sewn to perfection by our maker. We hold common threads of existence across time and space, existing in human form as well as in divine form. This link strengthens our bond and our ability to hold compassion for ourselves and others.

When you need to remember the commonality of life we all share, use the following affirmation from Jesus. He liked to affirm the beauty in each person he met. By seeing the light of truth within others, Jesus found that he could hold greater levels of compassion for them.

The Beauty of Life Within Affirmation

> I see the beauty of you,
> God's great gift to me,
> I love within you what God gave to me.

Forgiveness of the Master

Laughter rang out in the barren land, awakening Jesus from a deep sleep under a tree. Night had fallen, and Jesus realized that he had fallen asleep while meditating. Scratching his head, he realized that a sound had awoken him.

He scanned his surroundings but did not detect any movement. He shifted to his inner eyes and looked again.

"Ah, there you are," he said with a chuckle. He spied Quan Yin, the Chinese goddess of compassion, hovering over a rock in front of him. "Hello, dear one, do you have news for me?"

Quan Yin smiled and moved to sit next to him. "I bring you a message of love to pass on to your fellow beings."

Jesus smiled and said, "Please, tell."

"Not tell, but show today," she said, placing her hand between his shoulder blades. Suddenly he felt propelled into the heavens, and yet he had not left the ground. He could see clouds moving past him while he sat under the tree. His eyes shifted, and he began to see the divine world clearly around him. The desert landscape faded into the background while a bright, luminescent world of tranquillity materialized in front of him. He could hear water rushing by and realized that a waterfall of sound and color lay before him. Quan Yin, surrounded by a clear, beautiful pink light, moved slowly in circles. Knees bent, arms resting behind her back, she gently stepped in rhythm to the falling water.

Mesmerized by her movements, Jesus found himself up on his feet, following her steps. As he danced, he could hear the water music more clearly. He began to pick out different tones within the music, first, a low, continuous beat beneath all the other sounds. Then a tinkling sound, like bells ringing softly. And a chorus of voices, chanting in harmony within the other sounds. "All one, all one, all one," the chorus sang over and over again.

As he continued the dance, Jesus sensed that each sound held great energy. The low, continuous beat began to move through him, and he was moved to tears by the intensity of love he felt. The love settled deep within his body, filling every part of his being. Then the bells began ringing louder, and with each tone, he felt a great potential growing within him. He felt as if God's strength and compassion were his own, and he knew that he could achieve anything in that moment.

The chorus swelled, and he began chanting, "All one, all one, all one."

In that moment, he knew that he held God's forgiveness, great and abundant in his heart.

"In your father's house, there are many. But among the many, only one sound may be heard. It is the sound of one voice, one heart, one life. There are many flavors within the elixir of life, but we all drink from the same cup. The breath of life is the same breath of all," Quan Yin said, as she slowly moved to the music of life.

Just like Jesus, we too can experience the power of masterful living. Love builds the foundation for compassion to flow forth from your being, igniting your power of forgiveness. Forgiveness has been equated with divinity because to forgive, you need to access your mastery qualities of love and compassion. In love, you are able to see yourself and others as God sees us: beautiful beings on a journey of self-exploration and growth through the performance of a divine plan. With compassion, you believe that the greater potential of God can be expressed through others. By believing in this God-potential within all people, you can forgive the actions of yourself and others that fall short of the highest and best.

Hear now as God explains how to access the mastery quality of forgiveness:

Dear ones, explorers are searching for keys to themselves, trying on new jewels or behaviors they find in the treasure chest of their being. In exploration, some jewels are not flattering and may hurt the eyes of others. When we hurt others, we are showing a part of ourselves that hurts within us. This jewel, or behavior, is a reflection of an unresolved issue within us. We carry this issue around, and it surfaces when the pain is set off by an experience. Pain drives us to do things that we later regret. We all create painful situations for ourselves and others. We all have caused pain as well as received pain in our lives. Forgiveness is the recognition that pain happens in our lives, but it does not define who we are.

When we label those who hurt us as "bad," we have limited their potential. If we have no compassion for the bad, our love for them is compromised or diminished. Return to the foundation of love for all, compassion for all, and forgiveness flows for all. We forgive to allow ourselves to move on and not become stuck in the experiences of life. Experiences do not define who we are. At our very core, we are eternal beings of love having experiences in a human life. Recognize the love within those who hurt you, hold compassion for the commonality of your existence, and let the pain of the experience go through forgiveness. Forgive fully and freely, and then forget. Forgetting the offense means you hold the person in a state of ready compassion, recognizing the potential for greatness within this being. Forgetting the offense does not mean that you open yourself up to be hurt by others. Forgiveness allows you to honorably decide how you will continue in your relationship with this person.

You recognize the potential for greatness within yourself and others when you forgive. Forgiveness is love and compassion in action. Forgiveness is strongly linked with grace because it allows you to continue moving forward on your journey without carrying the pain of old experiences. When Jesus forgave the hurtful behavior of himself and others, he would hold all parties involved in prayer. Sometimes he would pray for days until he held forgiveness strong and full in his heart, which allowed others to receive this great gift of abundance from him. When he then forgave others in person, he let this gift flow freely from him. In the process of flowing forgiveness out of his being, the experience came to completion, and he did not look back upon it again. When you need to forgive yourself and others, use this powerful prayer method. You may pray for as long as you need until you are full of forgiveness and ready to release the experience.

The Prayer of Forgiveness

Dear God, I hold your abundance within me. In love, in compassion, I look upon those who have hurt me. Through your eyes, Lord, I see how this being was lovingly created by you, just as I am. Through your power, I choose to hold this being in love and compassion. I choose to forgive the pain they have caused by their choices. I choose to forgive myself for the pain I have caused by my choices. In honor, in love, I release the pain of this experience to continue upon my journey.

Personal Responsibility of the Master

As a master of your world, you make choices in how to live your life. When things go well, we feel good in taking credit for our decisions. When the outcome is poor, we may wish to spread blame among others for a situation we don't like. It can be a challenge to be responsible for your choices in all situations, and that is what makes personal responsibility an important mastery quality.

In his work as the Messiah, Jesus was responsible for his own actions. When he recruited his twelve disciples, he became responsible for their education on living a Spirit-driven life. He took on the charge of showing them by example, as well as by teaching them, how to present this new way of living through the power of God. He was a teacher, and he structured his life around this role. He presented information in a simple way that shook up and awoke the people he met. He took personal responsibility for what he taught, and his behavior among the people and the choices he made demonstrated to others the tangible presence of God in the world.

But Jesus' personal responsibility did not extend to the actions of others in his group. When a disciple acted poorly, making choices that did not benefit others, Jesus did not take responsibility for that person's behavior. When a disciple reached out in love to another person, Jesus did not take responsibility for that person's behavior. Jesus chose to teach others, and his disciples chose to follow his teachings. Along the path with these twelve men, one chose not to follow the teachings of Jesus. This disciple, Judas Iscariot, chose to follow another path by turning Jesus in to Jewish authorities.

Does Jesus' personal responsibility extend to the actions of Judas? Did Jesus fail as a teacher, making him partly responsible for Judas' actions, and ultimately, his own death?

Hear now as Jesus explains the power of personal responsibility:

Dear ones, we all make choices in life. We choose to get up in the morning and face the day despite the hardships we may endure. Dealing with other people can be one of the most challenging adventures you will take in life. We are so intertwined with our friends and family that sometimes we lose our boundaries. We may overstep with one another, doing things that would be better left for the other person to do on his or her own. We may blame ourselves for the short-comings of others, wondering how things might have been different if we had done more.

Personal responsibility comes with built-in boundaries of respect and honor. When we take responsibility for our own choices and actions, we are better able to sort out what is ours to hold and what is the responsibility of others in the event. We understand that in this life, others may make choices that hurt us. In taking personal responsibility, we look at all events in our life, including times when we hurt others as well as moments when we were wounded. A master recognizes his role and choices in both types of events.

In my life, I chose to become the Messiah. Through my divine connection, I learned of my role, and I made the decision to boldly move forward using the strength and power of God to do his work upon Earth. I chose twelve disciples, and I chose Judas to be my treasurer. As signs of my impending betrayal became apparent, I chose to let Judas know that I was aware of his choice to turn me over to the authorities. I chose to let him make his decision, knowing that I knew about his plan. When others choose a course that will hurt others, they are using the same energy that we use when we choose to show love to others. We live in God's world, and we use God's energy to create our world. Only God is present in God's world, and only people are responsible for the choices they make in using the creative power available to us all. I could have fought Judas's choice, or I could choose to allow it to occur. It was within God's plan, so it occurred.

In taking personal responsibility for my life on Earth, I am responsible for my own choice to allow a betrayal that I knew was imminent. I am responsible for bringing forth great words of wisdom from God to give comfort, grace, and love to his beautiful creations on Earth. I am responsible for the power and strength that I was lovingly given by God to do his work upon Earth. In taking responsibility, I let Judas and others hold the responsibility for the choices they made in life. I allow them the freedom to explore the outcomes of their choices, just as I have mine. I hold no regrets or anger toward these men, for I alone made my choices within my divine plan, just as they made theirs. In the land of the eternal heart, we are forever united in love, and I hold no experience over another. My heart of love runs deep for all I have touched while on Earth and through the veil.

Taking personal responsibility for your own choices and allowing others to hold their own requires courage and strength. This mastery quality moves beyond blame, anger, and regret about the outcome. It moves the event to the final step, which is a time of personal accounting for what has occurred. In the remembrance mastery plan model, this accounting takes place through reconnection. By remembering our eternal connection with one another and our inherent divinity, we can see beyond labeling each other as good or bad in the situation, moving instead to taking personal responsibility and accountability for our actions.

Just like Jesus, we can come to a place where we love with respect, allowing ourselves and others to be responsible for our choices and path in life. Jesus was clear on the responsibility he had in his life, but there were other people affected by the outcome of his choices. Mary was deeply affected by the death of Jesus, and she had to come to terms with the choices of those involved.

Hear now as Mother Mary shares how to take personal responsibility for your actions and behavior:

Dear ones, the heart of humanity beats as one. You all hold magnificent energy for producing incredible displays of creativity. You also hold fear within you that keeps you from extending that creative energy to others in order to resolve and release problems among you. Fear keeps us from reaching out to others and letting the pain go. I forgave the men who played a part in the death of my son because deep down they did not know what they were doing. They reacted unconsciously to the apparent threat of the Messiah, and in their sleeping state, they concocted a plan to execute my son. If at some point they had looked upon their actions and noticed an incongruency in their behavior, they may have been able to awaken and change their minds.

Noticing that your behavior hurts others even when your intentions are good may force you to see that your actions are incongruent with your intentions. If you can take this one step further and become conscious of your own behavior and its effect upon others, you are on the road to becoming a responsible being. In this responsibility, you become a master of your world, for you are conscious and awake, and you know who and what you are in this world and in the divine. Strive to become conscious, strive to awaken and claim personal responsibility in this life. This is the key to understanding others around you and accepting them as your brothers and sisters on this journey.

Personal responsibility pushes us to think beyond our normal way of dealing with others and become more than we are alone in any given moment. Jesus would ask himself a series of questions after an event occurred to better understand his role and responsibility. These questions set up a responsibility framework, which helped him to honor and respect the other people involved in the situation. He would use these personal responsibility questions during meditation, asking for help from his divine team when the answers were not clear-cut. Use the following personal responsibility meditation for both easy and difficult situations. This type of interaction with your divine team will strengthen your ability to consciously take personal responsibility for any situation.

Personal Responsibility Meditation

Find a quiet spot where you may speak out loud without being disturbed. You may wish to use pen and paper later in the meditation, so chose a place to sit where you may write comfortably. Close your eyes and breathe deeply. On each inhalation, see white light flowing into your body. Notice how the light is filling up every inch within your being. You feel warm and loved, secure within the world.

In this place of total acceptance, call out to your divine team by saying, *Divine guides, come to me now to provide love, assurance, and guidance. Hold me in the light of truth so that I may become a master of personal responsibility.*

See your divine team enter your space. Divine white light flows out from their forms, touching and opening your heart of love. Now let go of the pain of the situation you wish to explore by saying, *God, take my pain away. I willingly release this burden to you. In return, I willingly accept my divine wisdom and accountability. I choose now to take personal responsibility for this situation.*

Now ask yourself the following sets of personal responsibility questions. Allow your thoughts and feelings, as well as those of your divine team, to surface, helping you to come to a place of personal responsibility. You may write down the information if you wish.

1. What pains me about this situation?
    ✢ For which choices in the situation am I
      personally responsible?

THE JESUS PATH

2. What pains the other person about this situation?
   ✣ For which choices in the situation am I
      personally responsible?
3. How could I have handled the situation differently?
   ✣ For which choices in the situation am I
      personally responsible?

When you have reached a place of personal responsibility, see a silvery blue light fill your body. Let this light of truth fill you with the power to live in a mastery state of personal responsibility.

Recognizing Mastery in Your World

"Master, show me what you know," Jesus said to the shimmering being in front of him.

Sitting on the ground in a secluded grove of trees, Jesus gazed in wonder upon the etheric master. This glowing being wore white flowing robes and held a staff in his hands. His white hair was as long as his beard. The energy around him was palpable, and Jesus could feel it tingle upon his hand when he reached out to this master, Moses.

Kneeling down so that his forehead touched Jesus', Moses began to impart the wisdom he had gained through the ages. Jesus was immediately transported back in time. He could see Moses as the powerful man who led the people of Israel out of Egypt, the prophet who spoke of God as if he himself knew him, and a humanitarian, full of love and compassion for those in suffering around him.

218

As Moses sat back, Jesus looked upon him again with wonder. "I have read and been told about the greatness of your being, but I did not truly know you as myself until you shared your journey with me in this moment."

"A wise man knows that a piece of himself exists in all others in every moment," Moses said. "I am one with you in that you hold my peace within when you continue my work and the work of those before me. We all work in harmony and continue the stream of energy that can move the world to a place of peace. You are propelled by my work as I was propelled by the energy of those before me. We are all linked by the work we do in service of God."

Jesus accepted that to be an instrument of God, he would have to let go of his fears of being a tangible piece of God in the world for others to touch, hear, see, and know. Mastery of your divine plan requires that you let go of all pretenses of who you are. When you align your will with God's to actualize your plan, your mastery qualities begin to flow into you, providing the energy and skills needed to live a life filled with divine purpose.

At this point, your energy of mastery becomes fueled by the work of past instruments of God on Earth. Saints, prophets, masters, and other loving people of God have already put forth strong intentions, solid plans, tangible work, and great prayers for God's love and peace to manifest in our world. You add to this resource of energy as well as pull from it to support your own divine work. Whether you are exploring or performing your divine purpose, this mastery energy propels you forward.

Keys to accessing your mastery qualities are everywhere, and it takes a master to recognize the insights relevant to your own life. The Bible provides many tenets for living a life of devotion to God. Recent works on spirituality make contemporary many of the same tenets. As a master, you become a connoisseur of messages that speak to your heart, finding the wisdom that will move you forward on your path.

Messengers also come in the form of people we know and meet in planned and chance encounters. When we listen on a deeper level to what is being said in our conversations, we may find that others have been guided, consciously and unconsciously, to remind us how to achieve our divine plan. Listen to the words flowing into your consciousness every day, and you'll find keys and answers to your questions about living a masterful life. As a messenger, Jesus often spoke to people using strong, short statements that would stir up their hearts and minds, pushing them to look deeper at the world around them and their own role in it. It was the responsibility of each masterful person he encountered to truly hear the message and allow it to transform his or her life.

9

Step Seven:
Influencing Others for
the Common Good

WHILE traveling upon an empty stretch of road through the hot desert, Jesus sought out the shade of a large rock outcropping to rest his feet. As he walked around the rock to the shady side, he came face to face with a Roman spear, held by a young man.

Putting his hands up, Jesus said, "I come in peace, my friend. I am only seeking refuge from the sun."

"This refuge is taken," the Roman soldier said, jabbing at Jesus' chest.

Looking behind the soldier, Jesus noticed a young woman of Israeli heritage. She pulled her scarves closer around her face.

Enraged, the soldier yelled, "You must die for your impudence."

The soldier raised his spear to strike, but Jesus calmly held up his hand. The man took pause, momentarily dumbfounded by the peace emanating from Jesus.

"My time is near, dear friend, but I will not die by your tool," he said with a small smile.

The soldier lowered his weapon and said, "I cannot let you leave here alive knowing what you have seen."

"What have I seen but love itself?" Jesus asked, as he lay down in the shade by the man. "I will rest for a while and then be on my way."

Like Jesus, we have the opportunity to touch the hearts of others in any experience we encounter. But to help others, we have to help ourselves first. Using the divine model of awakening, you have learned how to hold a greater understanding of the world and your place in it. Through building a personal daily practice of connection to Spirit, you have explored how to release personal chains, reconnect with your higher spirit-self, disconnect from conventional wisdom, link with a higher source of energy, discover your divine purpose, and access your mastery qualities. Now that you have begun this work of clearing out old pain blocking your connection with God, you are ready to influence others to begin their own journeys home to the divine.

Jesus used his mastery qualities of love, compassion, forgiveness, and personal responsibility to influence and move others toward remembering their own inner greatness. Through his own way of life, Jesus showed others how to live in deep communion with God. Just by being himself, he changed the hearts of others.

Hear now as God explains how to remember your inner greatness and affect others by your choice to reconnect with Spirit:

Dear children, you come to Earth to experience life in seeming separation from all that you know. Here in this land of physicality, you learn many things and experience great pain. But through this pain, great growth and understanding are possible. All of these experiences are returned to me when you release the pain of these experiences. This energy flows back to me and becomes a part of the divine mass consciousness. Within this great consciousness, all moments are held and the learnings benefit all.

It is time to return the energy from your experiences to the greater consciousness of the divine source. As you let go of the old energy of this limited earthly life, you begin to open your awareness to the divine knowledge that is uniquely your own. This new energy flows freely into your human body as you tap into the unlimited source of knowledge of your higher spirit-self. You become an instrument of the divine, helping others to let go and receive kernels of truth.

In this moment, we are moving toward a unified existence of the divine and earthly realms, removing the veils of separation and again moving together as one being. Reclaim now who you truly are. Be not afraid to remember the greatness of your being, my child, my master of the universe.

Jesus used his divine knowledge, and by tapping into this source, he was able to view those who were deemed as outcasts of society instead as human beings, worthy of his compassion and love. Even if a person had bleeding blisters, parasitic infections, or bruises inside and out, Jesus never shrank from reaching out to others on their paths. These were only physical manifestations of a painful life, not the true reflection of the divine being residing within each person he touched. Jesus did not see just the human self of the people he met. He saw the divine self, the grand master who chose to have this experience in order to learn and grow. He knew that by touching people in a certain way, he would provide a roadmap to remembrance.

Jesus left many different keys of remembrance during his time on Earth, but all of his messages held a common theme: Help yourself first, and then help others on their paths. It is a part of our nature to help others and to show abundance. In the divine realm, beings work toward the greater good of all. In this environment of clear, open communication, divine beings share a world of love, generosity, abundance, and creativity. This is who we are at our core, and this expression of love toward others is one of the highest forms of divine creativity in action in our world today.

Looking Past Pain to Help Others

During our lives we can go through many trials and tribulations that seem huge, insurmountable, and unending. Painful events can become the pillars of our existence, and we may relate to others based on the physical, emotional, mental, and spiritual effects of these events on our lives. When you reach out to help another person, you have to see past your own issues to relate on a whole new level, free from judgment, anger, or other fear-based motives. Understanding how pain shapes us is important when you want to help others.

Many painful situations have touched us and others in our life: losing a loved one, having a physical disease, experiencing racism, surviving a violent crime, or losing a job can make us feel less than whole. When we experience painful situations, we may fear relationships with others and have difficulty trusting that their intentions are honorable. We may feel a lack of control in our lives and try to control others or become a doormat to the intentions of others. We may cite the painful event as a reason for the way our life has turned out. The painful event can overshadow our life, and we may feel like we will always be influenced by the painful memories and the subsequent behaviors we developed to continue through life. We can become the walking wounded and relate to others from a place of fear and pain rather than from power and love.

Hear now as God explains how these painful events change our energetic makeup:

Dear ones, all of us at one time or another in our lives will experience pain. But the way that we hold on to the pain determines how we walk through life. Many of us wear the victim label well. It is accepted in the world to be hurt and to limp through the rest of life, valiantly trying to piece life back together. And many of us do learn much about compassion, love, and forgiveness in going through this type of event. But this pain does not define who we truly are. We are not the walking wounded. We are courageous beings who are able to let go of pain and transcend the seemingly insurmountable problems in our lives.

When we lose a loved one in our life, be it to physical death or a change in partners, we feel hurt, betrayed, and alone. It is natural to feel this, as we are sentient beings. But at a certain point, that pain and its lesson are complete, and it can be released. This applies to all painful events in our lives: learn from them and then let them go. Do not carry the torch for energy that inhibits your natural grace and love.

When we feel hurt, we tend to physically shut down and close ourselves off from the world and other perceived sources of pain. We become small, closed beings acting out of self-protection and the fear of being hurt again. But we do not serve ourselves well by living as open wounds. The original pain energy becomes larger over time as we continually invest energy in keeping it alive, adding in new perceived pain sources related to the original source of hurt. Pretty soon, all incoming stimuli become a potential threat to our safety. We become a mound of fear and pain, functioning on a very low level. We are no longer just the victim of a painful event. We become victimizers of ourselves through our own victim energies.

Living in a brutal ancient society, Jesus saw firsthand how victims, often on the lower rungs of society, could perpetuate their victim status. Heads down, they did not see themselves as anything more. Today, we all hold some part of us that identifies with the victim. In childhood, our parents could make decisions for us, and oftentimes we couldn't change the situation. On some level, we developed an understanding of how victimization works. Lack of power over the self leads to feelings of victimization. It is this understanding of pain and feelings of victimization that create a common bond among all people.

When you can see the commonality of all experiences, you can hold compassion for other people and help them from a place of love rather than judgment. Jesus knew pain from his own life experiences, and he understood victimization well from living in the difficult world of ancient Israel. He knew firsthand from working with his father how hard it could be to provide for a family's survival. But he also knew how to let go of the pain of survival and tap into a greater power for living his life. When Jesus reached out to other people, he became a mirror for them to look at the situation through his response. He spoke openly about life issues facing them, giving them insight into the situation. He then showed them another way of living within the grace of Spirit, reflecting their potential for greatness through his own experience of connection with God.

Reaching out to others in a way that respects their mastery is a part of a process of mastering your own life issues. We cannot provide to others what we do not have in our own lives. We need to hold feelings of mastery within ourselves in order to project them out into the world. Jesus was a living example of mastery and when he touched others, he shared this mastery.

Hear now as Jesus explains how to become a mirror of truth:

Dear friends, we all want to help others in our life. We see someone in pain, and we want to take it away. We don't wish people to suffer, so we want them to move beyond these limiting situations. There are certain things that we can offer when we reach out to another person and other things that are not within our responsibility.

When you reach out to help other people, you cannot take their pain away. Only they can make the choice to let go of the hurt. We cannot live other people's lives for them. The goal is not to take their pain away. The goal of any interaction with other people is to provide a mirror for their behavior. By being honest about the effect of other people's behavior on you, you show them how much their intentions affect the outcome of their actions. If they don't intend for something to happen, but it always does, it is an opportunity for them to see that they are not in control of their behavior. Instead of flying manually and consciously, totally aware of their behavior and what is driving their actions, they are on autopilot.

All we can do for other people is to hold up the mirror. They must decide what to do. It is their choice to do something new, not ours. We may make choices in response to other people's decisions not to change a behavior. If we find the behavior hurtful, we may choose how to proceed so that we will not be affected by their actions.

Life is about choice and about learning from the outcome of our choices through the reactions of those around us. We see and understand our behavior by how others respond to us. We cannot force change upon other people. We can only honestly reflect to them how their behavior affects us and allow them the grace to let those behaviors go.

Jesus reflected to the ancient people of Israel the outcome of their behavior. The mistreatment of poor and sick people by Jewish leaders created a situation of scarcity and persecution among people in that society. Strict religious laws, upheld by Jewish leaders, created a religious caste system where only the rich and privileged were seen as worthy of the grace of God. The temple, once a symbol of God, became a symbol of wealth and commerce. All of Jesus' actions mirrored the effect of these societal behaviors on the common people of ancient Israel. And in holding up the mirror, Jesus gave people an opportunity to choose another way of living: through the power of God's acceptance and love of all people.

To become a mirror for change as Jesus did, you have to be clear on your own motives. Jesus would use a mirror tool to better understand how to honestly reflect to others the effect of their behavior. He had to release his pain and anger first before he could be an open reflection, free of judgment and anger. People will only look into a mirror if they feel that the reflection holds truth. Coming from a place of compassion and love, Jesus would use parables, metaphors, humor, and strong statements to describe the situation and not necessarily the person. He allowed others the choice to take in the information and use it to change their own life. Use the following mirror tool to let go of your pain in the situation and become a true reflection for other people.

Mirror of Compassion Tool

When you encounter a situation that has caused you pain, first review and release your own issues, and then talk to the other parties involved. In using this tool, you will find that the mirror also reflects back your own issues, offering you an opportunity to choose growth and reconnection with Spirit as well. Before using the mirror tool, it may be helpful to do the personal responsibility meditation in chapter 8 so that you are clear on your role in the situation.

Consciously ask your divine team to assist you by saying, *Divine team, be with me now to illuminate this experience with the light of truth. Help me to release this pain and gain clarity in the situation.* Take a moment to answer the following questions.

1. What am I feeling as a result of this experience?
2. Which feelings are related to this current experience?
3. Which feelings are related to old energy I carry from past experiences in my own life?
4. What pattern do I carry that allows me to continually encounter this type of experience?

Now that you understand your feelings, release the pain of the present and past situations. Close your eyes, and breathe deeply. See a bright white light enter your crown, filling your body quickly. The light finds the pain in your being and wraps around it like a puffy cloud. Now say, *I willingly release this pain. I choose not to hold this energy in my being.* A white funnel opens above your head, and the white cloud puffs are pulled out of your body. A silvery-blue light of truth then flows into your crown, filling your body completely.

Now it is time to hold up a mirror to this experience.

Visualize a large mirror in front of you, extending from the
floor to the ceiling, surrounded by white light. Walk in front
of this mirror, and say, *I choose to live in the light of truth.
Show me why I encounter these types of experiences.* Allow any
thoughts, feelings, or images to appear in the mirror. Let the
information flow into your consciousness without judgment.

When the information is complete, look into the mirror
and say, *I choose to be a mirror for others involved in this situation. Through the loving light of truth, how may I compassion-
ately reflect this situation to others?* You may ask questions to
clarify the guidance.

When you feel complete, open your eyes knowing that
you can connect with others through the power of compassion and love.

Choices of the Master

"Shh, be quiet," the disciple whispered to the man beside him as
they crept through the wilderness to a house with a large courtyard. People were eating and laughing, enjoying the company of
Jesus. Hidden behind bushes, the disciple and the man could see
Jesus speaking to a group of women.

"Doesn't he know that women should not be involved in
higher learning?" the man whispered to the disciple, who in
turn motioned for him to be quiet.

Soon the women left Jesus' side, and he was joined by a group
of his disciples.

"Master, we want you to preach in Jerusalem where more

people can hear God's word," said the disciple closest to Jesus.

The man in the bushes turned to his consort with an angry look, and muttered, "God's word indeed. Blasphemy!"

Again, the disciple motioned for him to be silent.

"All in good time, my dear friends. We will go to Jerusalem when my father is ready," Jesus said.

He looked at the group and said, "I see eleven here, we are missing one."

"We are always missing one," some of the disciples muttered.

In the bushes, the missing disciple and the man looked at each other in alarm.

"We all have our paths to walk, and each one must be honored," Jesus said. "I love you all greatly, whether you accept my love or not. My love for you is not diminished by your actions, whether great or small."

The missing disciple turned his eyes downward as the group continued their conversation.

Like Jesus, each of us has chosen a path to walk upon in this world. Jesus chose to be an instrument of God, honoring the role of the divine in our world. He knew that his road would not be easy and would require a violent ending in order to show the world that life is eternal. Others of his time also chose their paths. Some, like Judas, also played difficult roles that would forever place them in infamy in the minds of the living.

But to God, all actions and outcomes are the same. All actions produce energetic effects, and this energy can be released. We all have caused pain to other people during our lifetimes, but God holds no scorecard or permanent record of our misdoings. When God says to release old energy back to him, it is no longer our property. In letting go of the pain, forgiveness is a given part of the exchange, for we did not know what we did. For if we were conscious, like our higher spirit-self, we would take responsibility for our actions and think before we do things. We are often on autopilot, and we act without thinking.

For some, like Judas, their deeds became a part of a greater plan.

Hear now as God explains the roles we choose in life:

Dear ones, during the time of Jesus, many divine beings in human form took on roles to better illustrate the meaning of love and abundance. Judas, a loving spirit, took on the diffi-cult role of persecuting the Messiah. His higher spirit-self was aware of Judas's impending actions of betrayal, but these actions were within the scope of my plan for the Messiah. Judas's higher spirit-self agreed to allow him to continue upon this course. But Judas, in his frail human form, did not know the import of his actions. He only acted out from his small life, which taught a greater lesson to all.

The shame of Judas's actions did not, however, follow him to the divine realm, for all energetic consequences are for-given. Upon his death by his own hand, Judas returned directly to the divine realm, where he was greatly supported and loved by all. Here he received abundant counsel to release the energetic pain of his actions and to grow from the experience. It takes a strong spirit to play such a big part in the story of the Messiah.

There are others in this world who have caused great pain to millions by carrying out racial massacres. These men were not asked to play a role in the Messiah story. Rather, they acted out of the ignorance of their own circumstances. These horrors play out, however, as a part of the earthly experience of separation. I do not turn my back on these injustices; rather I turn with greater love to these individuals who have lost their way. There is no "hell" for these souls. Instead, they exist in a limbo state of pain where they fear my wrath. There's no wrath of God, only the loving embrace of energetic release. I say to you, my children, you are all equal in the divine realm. You will all return to the divine realm upon the completion of your earthly experience. You'll have abundant love and understanding to let the energetic consequences of your actions return to the source of all energy.

The journey for these tortured souls generally does not end with physical death. They float in limbo, confused and fearful. Upon their guided return home by loving angels, they are given abundant love, energy, and counsel. But they must accept this help, let go of the pain, and return to a full state of connection with their higher spirit-self. Often the trauma of such a tortured existence causes a temporary break with the higher spirit-self, and this soul must gently let go of the pain and reestablish this link. Because the earthly realm still exists, we allow these souls time to reestablish their link and fully learn from their experience on Earth. Some return to Earth, some do not, depending on what that soul and I have planned and whether another lifetime would amend the karmic repercussions of past lives.

Know this and this alone: no one is lost from my sight. All lives are carefully planned and monitored by me and higher spirit-selves, angels, and ascended beings. All experiences in this realm of separation are valid, for they represent what can occur in a state of separation from the divine. Because this earthly realm is a place of learning, all events and actions are forgiven, for they truly do not represent who you are in the divine realm: a masterful divine being. Take away a man's glasses, and he may walk off a cliff, knock over a child, or fall down. Restore him to his full capacity of being, and he behaves in a very different manner. But judge not, hate not, fear not who the man was in his weakened state, for that is not who the man truly is. Honor, love, and hold compassion for your blind brothers and sisters, knowing that they truly do not know the import of their actions, for they truly do not know and accept their true essence. It is only through love that you may truly know yourself and your brothers and sisters.

We all choose our path, consciously and unconsciously, to walk in life. Looking back at each turning point in our life, we may remember a key piece of information that came to our attention at that time. In this choice point, we were given what we needed to make a decision. When Jesus began his journey out into the world to touch hearts, he had a choice moment with his father, Joseph. He feared Joseph's disapproval of his chosen ministry. In that moment, Jesus received divine knowledge that his father wished only the highest and best for him and that he could move forward with his father's blessing. Jesus received this information through his spiritual connection, which he confirmed with his father. In that choice moment, Jesus had all that he needed to move forward confidently. He recognized the moment and the choices he had, and he chose to step forward as a man of God.

These choice points are revealed in every moment of our lives. Some are big, and some are small, but we always hold the power of choice in our experiences. It takes a master to recognize the choices around us. Only a master who looks for options and the power of choice can influence others to view life in the same way. Through Jesus, Judas experienced a choice point. Even though Judas hid in the bushes of betrayal, the master still reached out to him with love and compassion. Through his lesson with the other disciples in the courtyard, Jesus showed Judas that he held the power of choice in all of his deeds. Only Judas could make the final decision to betray Jesus.

A master brings many gifts to others, and one of the greatest is recognizing the power of choice we all possess. Jesus was a master of his choices and experiences, but he was not a master over others. He recognized that we all hold the power to choose experiences, reactions, actions, emotions, feelings, and thoughts to drive our existence. Each master painter holds his or her brush of choice in different ways. Some use bold strokes, splattering paint on those around them. Others use delicate movements, staying within the canvas. And some lay down the brush, never realizing that creation needs to be done. We are the master painters of our own lives, and we choose how to create our masterpieces.

As master painters of creation, we each hold a little can of paint, taken from God's abundant supply. We are a smaller version of God's world of creation, and we can create on a small scale in this earthly realm of experience. Each choice point in our life acts like a moment of creation in the following ways:

- *Free will.* Our little can of paint holds our free will, which represents our creative energy store of potential possibilities that we will choose to create in our lives.
- *Potential possibilities.* When you dip your paintbrush into your little can of possibilities, you may choose to create many realities, and some may be different from your divine plan.
- *Separate realities.* As you lay your brush upon the canvas of your life, your thoughts, emotions, feelings, and actions act like the bristles on the brush, creating realities separate from your divine plan. Using your little disconnected can of creation, these separate realities often do not reflect the essence of your higher spirit-self. The energies and experiences of your life are often not a true reflection of your divine plan.
- *Divine plan.* As master painters, when we decide to pull from a greater source of creation, we access the power of our divine plan with God. The energy of the little

can of possibilities and separate realities merges back into God's great creation energy. Using our free will as master painters, we choose to create our divine plan on Earth through experiences that provide opportunities to choose greater reconnection with Spirit.

✤ *Heaven on Earth.* Through an open, loving connection with the God of our hearts, we become master creators and instruments of Spirit, letting the power and love of God illuminate the world through our choices.

As a master creator, if you accept the power of your choices, you accept the power others have over their choices. We are all responsible for our own creations, and a master allows others to experience the consequences of their actions, whether positive or negative. A master does not carry another master's brushes. We choose to give to others what God gives to us: free will to make choices and take responsibility for the outcome of these choices. Life is a choice experience.

Jesus made strong choices in his life, and he often had difficulty in remaining optimistic about the choices he made in relation to others. He genuinely loved people, so it was hard for him to let others take responsibility for their own actions. He worked on recognizing choices for what they truly are: our creative power from God. Knowing that free will to make creative choices is a gift from God, Jesus would give the same gift to others. He would remind himself to step back and not carry others by using the following affirmation to confirm everyone's power of choice.

The Choice of Love Affirmation

I choose to love you in this moment.

My heart holds God's love for your choices.

Master, I see God's love in you.

With honor and love, I choose to let you be the master
of your life.

Seeing the Christ in Others

"Look into my eyes, and know that I am one within you," Jesus
said to eleven of his disciples, who were seated in a circle around
him under the night sky. The men had just shared a meal
together and had retreated to the hills for privacy.

The disciples looked at Jesus in confusion. His words seemed
so poetic and beautiful, but oftentimes they took his sayings as
fanciful suggestions.

"Truly, I say to you, look into my eyes," he said, motioning
for the group to move closer and peer into his eyes. Hesitantly,
the men moved in so that each had a clear view of Jesus' face.
Calmly, Jesus stared forward. Slowly, he began looking deeply at
each disciple. His first disciple laughed a little as Jesus stared at
him intently.

"Settle, my friend," Jesus said to him. "Breathe with my
breath and truly feel the oneness with me."

The disciple took a deep breath and looked at Jesus in
earnest. Together, the men synchronized their breathing. The
man felt locked in the gaze of Jesus. As he looked deeply into the

eyes of the master, he felt all of his cares slowly slipping away. He felt as if he were floating above the ground, buoyed up by the powerful energy emanating from Jesus' eyes.

"Remember this moment always," he said after he had shared his soul with each man present in the circle. "I am always within you, within each breath you take, within each thought you have, within each moment you walk this heavenly path. You are never alone. Remember this always."

The disciples of Jesus have often been described as an unlikely group of leaders in bringing forth the good news of God. They were not wealthy or influential men. Rather, they were from the lower classes: some were fishermen, some were tag-alongs, some were traitors, and some were tax collectors. This unlikely group of men formed the core group of Jesus' confidants, men privy to Jesus' inner connection with God. Jesus shared firsthand with his disciples the teachings of God. By using the energy of Jesus' connection with the divine, these men were able to experience many of the same divine encounters as Jesus. After Jesus physically departed, the disciples practiced using his teachings as their own and opened their own strong connections with Spirit.

Today, many of us can relate to the unrefined character of the disciples. Many of us feel lost, mired down by the mistakes we have made. We may feel unworthy of God's love and fear that we don't have the skills within us to live as Jesus did and to walk in his footsteps. In many ways, we are the living disciples of Jesus because he took the common man and elevated him to a state of Christhood. Each of us holds the energy of Jesus, for we all hold the essence of God within. It is this commonality of energy that propels us upon the path in the footsteps of Christ.

It is in this commonality that we can see the divine in others. We all have laid aside our fine robes to get down in the mud of life. And in this experience of the basest of emotions, we see sides of ourselves that can make us feel shame. This blanket of shame covers us all, blinding us to the energy of divinity flowing through each and every one of us. Jesus taught his disciples to lift the blanket and search within the heart of others for that divine spark that burns within us all. It is in this commonality of energy that we begin to see the pureness and truth hidden within others. Within this divinity, this pure essence in us all, we dwell together in abundance and harmony.

Hear now as Jesus explains how to see others as their true divine selves:

Dear ones, your human self is connected to a divine higher spirit-self who resides in the divine realm, which is a level of consciousness slightly removed from your own earthly world. In the divine realm, you are never in want of anything. All you need is provided for you in abundance. In this realm of pure energy, you have the power to create incredible worlds of energy, and you have all the means needed to live in peace, happiness, and tranquillity.

In your earthly experience, you are learning what it is like to live in a world of limitations, a world where physicality rules the experience. With physicality and mass come limited resources to support your world. But you hold an abundance of energy within you, meaning you are linked energetically to your abundant higher spirit-self. Open your connection to your higher spirit-self, and you open your access to abundance. Everyone is capable of opening this connection and operating from a higher source of abundance. Seeing this divinity within everyone you meet frees you from competing with others. See others as a part of the abundance and give freely, for sharing the wealth of energy means that you also will receive an abundance of energy.

Coming from a place of abundance means that we can access unlimited energy and love. We are linked into a vast source of energy, which has the ability to manifest great things in our world. Strong intentions can actualize many things, but we also have the ability to directly influence the in-flow of divine energy that makes things happen in our world. Ask and you shall receive, Jesus once said to his disciples. Ask for divine love to flow through you, and you shall receive it abundantly to open your heart and the hearts of others around you.

Jesus found that by linking with God and his divine plan, an abundance of energy flowed freely through his being to make miracles happen. He did not hold that power when he was living as a carpenter's son, following in Joseph's footsteps. That power manifested itself through Jesus when he connected with his higher spirit-self and released old blocking energy. By becoming a clear, open instrument of God, Jesus allowed this divine energy to surge through his physical body and affect the world around him. His physical body, his human form, became a vessel for his divine self to work through. His higher spirit-self connected directly with the human body, breaking down all veils of separation between heaven and Earth within this one being called Jesus. In essence, Jesus actualized his divine plan within his human form.

When we become aware of the divine self within our human existence, we can see this light of God in everyone we meet. We can only recognize divinity in others when we accept it in ourselves. A master sees the light dwelling in others despite their unenlightened behavior. A master recognizes that in this world of experience, we are all seeking the light and clarity of our being. A master honors this common pursuit, compassionate and accepting of others and their choices.

At many points in their journey with Jesus, the disciples demonstrated unenlightened behavior. The disciples were not extraordinary men. They were regular, everyday people who experienced difficulties in practicing the teachings of Jesus. Their judgments of others, their anger and desire to solve issues with violence, and their fear of letting down these defenses weighed heavily upon their shoulders. They felt challenged in releasing these burdens and living as Jesus taught them. But through their interactions with Jesus, the disciples and the master learned to have compassion for each other and to recognize the greater light of divinity dwelling within. Laying aside frustrations and fear, the disciples and the master looked beyond the physical manifestations of pain and separation and chose to accept each other as divine beings on a path to greater actualization of their God-self in the world. In the light of acceptance, you can see others as a part of the great journey home.

As Jesus connected more with his higher spirit-self, he worked to spread this abundance of light energetically through the world. Just touching one heart with love makes a difference. Jesus used the following affirmation to ignite the light of love and divine understanding in others. He found that it changed hearts and awakened the divine within the people around him. He would silently bless the people he met, as well as hold others in prayer when he felt challenged in seeing their light of God within.

Heart of Love Affirmation

You, before me, are of me.
You, beside me, are within me.
You, behind me, are my essence.
Lovingly, knowingly, fully aware of your greatness,
I lift you up full in my arms.
You, great being of love and light, I honor you.
I love you for who you are, here and now.
Master, I lie down before you and offer my life for yours.
May my life show you the way home to who you are.
In abundance, in love, in peace, I am eternally your friend.

Actualizing Your Divine Plan to Influence Others

Jesus came to Earth with a mission, just as we have. In actualizing his divine plan, he became an example for others to follow. He touched millions of lives by his actions. Each of us holds a divine plan that will touch hearts in many different ways. Through exploration and performance of our divine plan, we change ourselves and others we meet.

Courage is a divine quality that moves us beyond fear to that moment when we know that we are truly instruments of God. In that knowingness, we recognize the grace and abundance we hold in all moments to rise above our small circumstances and make a difference in the lives of those around us. Courage enables us to touch the shoulder of a stranger in need of comfort. Courage moves us to leave an abusive relationship. Courage leads us down new paths of self-knowledge. Courage allows us to take personal responsibility for actions that have hurt others. Courage lets us live a divine life and actualize our divine plan, right here, right now.

Courage allowed Jesus to complete his divine plan on Earth and forever change our hearts.

"Let my peace be within you," God said to Jesus, as soldiers lashed out violently at his naked back. Using what little strength he had left, he momentarily stood up on his knees and embraced the love from his heavenly father.

The soldiers laughed. Pain again exploded in Jesus' body.

"Let peace fill you, know that you are loved," a beautiful angelic voice said to Jesus. "You are not alone, dear Jesus. The kingdom of God surrounds you."

Jesus felt a shift in his body, and his awareness became doubled. He could see his physical body being lifted and placed upon a cross, bound and tied. And yet he could not feel the sensations in his limbs.

Jesus realized that he was standing on the ground in front of his body on the cross. He was a glowing white being, and his robes were clean and flowing. His mother knelt at the base of the cross. He could hear her thoughts of pain, her silent lamentations.

The familiar physical world now looked very different. The dusty landscape was alive with color. Humans merged with the energy of the plants and earth, like a flowing, living watercolor painting.

"Look," Jesus said. "I am of this world, and yet I am not."

The skies turned stormy above his fallen body. Lightning flashed brilliantly, and fragments of light swirled around his body on the cross. The light entered his body, and his awareness was jolted back into his physical form.

"It is done," Jesus screamed as he felt himself wrenched from his body.

He was blinded by white light before realizing he no longer had eyes with which to see. He wanted to lift his arms to shield his eyes before realizing he no longer had a body to command and control.

In that moment, he realized that he was the light.

Soaring, swirling, moving in harmony and yet fully free, he spiraled out in all directions.

"I am all," he knew in that moment.

10

Living on a New Level of Consciousness

"WALK with me, dear one," the angel with the crown of flowers said to Jesus.

He didn't so much walk as float, suspended above a beautiful cloudy landscape of colors: blues, greens, reds, and purples—all of the colors flowed together in a moving symphony of sound, texture, and hue.

He glanced down at his body, but it didn't look the same. His body glowed with a brilliance he had not seen before. He looked like the sun, with rays of white light emanating from his being. He held up his hand, and golden beams of light flowed from his fingertips.

He could vaguely remember in that moment how he got to this place.

"Let it come slowly," said his guardian angel.

Her words were not spoken, but instead felt like vibrations directed within his being. When her words touched him, he felt the intention, emotion, and truth behind the words. Her simple words were just that: simple. They held no possibility for mis-understandings or duplicity. He knew in that moment that this angel loved him deeply, cared for his well-being with all of her heart, and only wanted the highest and best for him.

He stopped moving, and stared at her, awestruck.

"I know you with my heart and soul," he said, communicating with her in the same manner. "I know that we have been together for many a moment, helping and guiding each other. We are a team, a great team," he said, as joyful laughter burst throughout his being, leaving behind a shimmering dance of gold light.

In that moment of great remembering, Jesus and his angel danced together as two stars, two points of light in an infinite universe. Shimmering, glowing, swirling, moving in harmony, they shared the kind of joy that only old friends know.

"I remember it all now," Jesus said, slowing the dance of remembrance. "The great shift over . . . the walk of pain to the cross . . . the mock trial . . . the journey of faith . . . the beginning of life on Earth. And yet I am not finished with my plan. There is more, much more to do."

With that, he took his angel's hands and spun in circles through the colorful clouds.

"Let us begin again," he shouted with joy.

Living Heaven on Earth Now

In this moment, you have walked with Jesus on his path. You have experienced his emotions, his fears, his triumphs, and his glory of returning to the divine kingdom of God. His journey, while amazing and inspiring, is no greater than your own. We all come to Earth to explore and perform our divine plans through the experience of separation from God. We all hold within us the capability to shed our old skin and awake anew.

When you live within the divine model of awakening and transcend this world of fears, you reach a state of mastery: awareness of the coexistence of the earthly and divine realms. Jesus lived simultaneously within both worlds. He felt connected with the heart of God as well as with his fellow human beings. He was moved by God's love, allowing it to change how he viewed God's kingdom in heaven and on Earth. He allowed his senses to expand to encompass all of God's creative moments, from divine experiences of learning with masters and angels, to earthly lessons that tried his compassion and love in an environment of scarcity. He became more than just a man alone in life. He became the hand of God, reaching into a dark world to open the door to lightness again. He used this dual awareness not to transcend above life but to transcend into life. He became more a part of life and the lives of others by his choice to allow the richness and fullness of God's world to shine through him on Earth. He walked without fear of earthly laws and lived within God's laws of love, peace, faith, and tranquillity. He lived heaven on Earth, where the human being recognizes the divine order and power creating the earthly world of experience. In holding this dual awareness, the human being sees life as a rich opportunity for experiences that are designed to reawaken the soul and reconnect with the higher spirit-self.

Hear now as Mother Mary explains this journey to dual awareness:

Dear ones, now you know the story of Jesus and his journey. He demonstrated to all on Earth how to live not by the rules, but by the essence of truth. Rules are static and based on physical laws of immobility. Rules tell us not to talk to strangers, but in truth, we are all brothers and sisters. Rules tell us not to take candy from strangers, but in truth, we all exist to help others fully along their journey, be it to provide sustenance or assurance. Let not this world of rules shield you from your great journey.

Live not by the rules, but by the truth of the moment. Based on the rules, Jesus was not a "good" Jew. He flouted religious authority, vandalized the marketplace in the temple, healed the sick on holy days, and did not keep the strict laws of purity. He failed utterly under the rules of Judaism. But does the flaw lie within the man or within the rules? Based on the truth, Jesus worked hand-in-hand with the divine to bring forth the messages of God to the world. He showed religious authorities that their own rules were strangling the life out of men and women; he showed the mockery made of temples of worship, both internal and external to humans; he lifted the downtrodden to show others that wholeness is attainable; and he lived fully unafraid and unfettered by laws that constrict the divine flow of truth and love into the human creation.

Based on his life, Jesus showed humankind how to follow

the divine truth and not preconceived, man-made ideas of divinity. Religious rules are often a far cry from the truth of our divine selves. These rules are based on man-made limitations. We live in a world of scarcity and limitation, and these constrictions are reflected in our thoughts, views, and movement within the physical world. The divine realm is not based upon limitations. We exist within a world based upon abundance and mutual accord.

The truths of these worlds are very different and yet they are the same because we are the inhabitants of both worlds. This earthly realm is an extension of the divine realm. This extension is born of the need to explore and know ourselves through all experiences. So this experience of separation has generated many rigid rules based upon limitation. I say to you, dear ones, that your mission is to see past the physical and reclaim the divine world around you. To truly learn the lessons of Jesus, you need to truly live as Jesus did: aware of the two worlds he coexisted in. Take this to heart, dear ones, and draw strength from the master, Jesus. Let his step be your own. Let his strength and pursuit of the truth of his existence be your own. And most of all, let love guide you. For when we move from a place of love, the light of truth always shines. Blessed be my brothers and sisters, fully awake and aware of their own greatness.

Holding an awareness of both the divine and earthly realms changes how you view yourself and your interactions with others. When you see yourself as a part of a greater plan, the self-made and societal limitations constraining us can be released. You transcend your human limitations to merge with your higher spirit-self and expand your conscious awareness. In this expanded state, you hold the physical body of the human experience plus the spiritual wisdom of your enlightened self. In this powerful combination, you are forever connected with your divine strengths of love, compassion, and forgiveness, and you radiate these mastery qualities in all of your interactions with others. You walk as Jesus did, fully linked into your power in both realms.

Hear now as Jesus explains the link between the divine and earthly realms:

My friends, I know how alluring this earthly life can be in sheltering you from the truth of your existence. Many will tell you not to reconnect with the divine, that you cannot trust the validity of your own experience. Know now that you are the master of this link to the divine realm. You control the opening of this connection by your will and intention. Open this portal wide, and you can reclaim your divine grace while still in human form. You need not die physically to remember the greatness of your being. And herein lies the strength of this quest: In reconnecting with your higher spirit-self, you connect with your abundance. And through this abundance, you can achieve far greater things in this world than going it alone.

As you read my words, you hold a book in your hands. You recognize the words and you can process intellectually what I am saying. You relate well to the tangible in your world, the physical reminders of the solidity of life on Earth. You see yourself as a human being with a body that will begin to slow down and eventually die. But many don't know what happens to the body when we die. Where does your spirit go? How does this intricate web of life linking the earthly and divine realms work?

From my own journey, you have discovered that we are made from light energy. It fills every cell in our bodies, giving us energy to grow, fight disease, and eventually die. The light is all that we are. Your body is like a flashlight, holding the energy produced by battery cells. Turn on the flashlight, and the true essence of light shines forth. When the light leaves the flashlight, it is transported out of the torch by light waves. The waves flow out into the universe like ripples on a pond, touching and illuminating objects in its path, and finally disintegrating when the battery cells no longer produce energy or the switch is turned off.

The human body does not have rechargeable batteries, so when the energy supply of the body is completely spent, the human shell is no longer needed. The body is laid to rest, honored for housing the light energy, and enabling a divine being to experience life in human form. The divine being, the soul who dwelled within the human body, is set free from this limited existence. In a grand burst of light energy, the spirit shifts from this human consciousness to the divine consciousness, which is its natural state of being. The spirit is pure light energy, abundant and full of God's grace.

Returning to its place of divine origin, the journey continues from another level of consciousness. The life is reviewed and compared with the divine plan. Much laughter and love, tears and accountability for actions, and compassion and strength are generated during this time of review. Greater growth occurs during these moments as the spirit determines its next course of action. The great cycle of growth and experience in all forms continues uninterrupted throughout the infinite universe.

It is from this infinite source of being that I come to you now. You may not see or touch me in human form, but I still exist. We may not share a glass of wine, but I still exist. We may not break bread together, but I still exist. Life is eternal, dear friends, and I still exist. When you can accept that you are more than just this human body, you can accept the great abundance of God that makes this experience possible. Seeing yourself as an eternal, infinite being frees you from living a life of convention and limitation. See this journey as more than meets the eye, remembering your true mission upon Earth in this moment. Blessed ones, loved so completely and purely within my heart, step into the infinite now and take your place in both the Earth and divine realms.

Expanding Your Consciousness with the Divine Model of Awakening

After returning to the divine realm, Jesus' work on Earth was not done. Three days after being entombed, he completely reclaimed his divinity.

A great angel of light appeared outside of the tomb and removed the stone from the doorway.

"Praise the Lord, for his son is risen today. Go forth and tell others the good news of the coming of Christ in this world," the angel said to two men grieving by the tomb. Overcome with joy, the men rushed off to share the word of God with others.

A woman whom Jesus had saved from stoning then came upon the opened tomb. Falling to her knees, she began crying.

"Lord, why do they continue to dishonor you? Why must they commit this evil act of taking your body from its place of resting?" she cried out.

A gentle hand upon her shoulder momentarily stopped her lamentations. Glancing up at a man beside her, she continued to cry, "Why, tell me why they have taken the body of my Lord?"

"Cry not, dear woman, for your Lord is beside you," said Jesus, kneeling beside the woman and lifting her face to look into his own. "It is I, Jesus. I am always here with you."

Screaming out with joy, the woman stood and embraced Jesus. She felt a great warmth envelop her.

"My Lord, why is it that you seem real to me?" she asked, placing her hand within his.

"I am in my father's house, where love and abundance reign. Where no man goes hungry, no man strikes another. It is from this place of abundance that I come to you. You feel my warmth because you expect it. You feel my hand because you desire its embrace. You see and feel because your love for me is so great," Jesus said, gently brushing the hair away from the woman's face.

"You see and know me well, for I have always been here with you. I will always be here with you whether you can touch me or see me. Let your desire to be with me be strong. Let your hope for my touch be strong. Let your will to live as I do in this moment be strong, for you too can live as I do in my father's house."

Crying, the woman held Jesus' hand in her own and used it to wipe away her tears. As the drops touched his skin, they fluttered into his being, like doves in flight. The woman was not afraid, for in that moment she knew that Jesus was hope, faith, and peace standing before her.

"My love for you master, take it," she said, placing his hand upon her heart. Closing her eyes, she could feel her love flowing into the hand of the master. And just as the love flowed from her being, it was returned in great abundance as a golden warmth, more brilliant than the sun, more filling than the laughter of a child, more sweet than the embrace of a baby. She felt more loved than she ever had in her life.

"Remember this moment always," Jesus whispered to her. "Search for me everywhere—in the hills, in the rustling of the trees, in the song of the bird, in the sunlight upon your face. Seek out the peace of your heart, find the refuge where you and I are one of the heart. Always, always together in love in our father's house."

Gently placing his hands upon the woman's shoulders, Jesus said, "Go, my sister, go tell the others of the glories of God."

Laughing, the woman turned and ran to find the disciples of Jesus to share the good news.

Like the ancient people of Israel, we are touched by the blessings of God. These people felt Jesus' hand upon their shoulders, heard his words ringing in the temple courtyard, and knelt by his side to praise God. Today, the presence of Jesus is still very real in our world. When we go inside of our hearts through meditation and prayer, we can feel Jesus in ways that are just as real as our ancient counterparts felt two thousand years ago.

The divine model of awakening offers us a way to feel Jesus, know God, and remember our divine self. As we let our mastery qualities of love, compassion, forgiveness, and personal responsibility govern our lives, we begin to live from a place of expanded consciousness. In this expanded state, we pull from our infinite wisdom to live from a higher place of compassion for others and ourselves. We are able to love others freely based upon our commonalities, rather than from the desire to gain something or fill an emptiness inside. We can forgive others because we hold an abundance of compassion and love to share with ourselves and others. And we can take personal responsibility for our actions, great and small, positive and negative, and allow ourselves and others to walk unfettered by unrealistic expectations, unnecessary burdens, and desires that do not serve all involved. An expanded consciousness allows us to recognize that we chose this life experience to gain valuable insight into our core essence and to remember the missing pieces of life's puzzle: our higher spirit-self and our ever-present connection with God.

From the example of the life of Jesus, we know that it is possible to let God guide our actions and help us to touch the world on a deeper level. People were moved to tears by the words of Jesus, and many would find their hearts opening up even when he had only touched their hands. There is a place, deep within us, that yearns for that knowingness, that sense of belonging in the world. When others shun us, despise us, or mock us, we retreat like small animals into our dens, licking our wounds. We wonder if we can ever be loved for who we are. The life of Jesus reminds us that love exists beyond what we can experience in this earthly world. Love extends from the world of God, into our heart, and we only need to look inside to feel that eternal flame of belonging.

Expanding your consciousness allows you to tap into a place of wholeness, where vitality and strength are eternal. You exist right now as a whole being, free from pain, anger, scarcity, fear, and hopelessness. Your higher spirit-self is you on a higher level of awareness. Your human self holds blocks and blinders to the wonders of the world, both earthly and divine. Your higher spirit-self is your guide to letting this pain go and stepping completely into your chosen divine role. You have found the key to greatness: you already hold it within.

The divine model of awakening is designed to open your heart and allow your divine higher spirit-self to lead you home to your expanded consciousness. Your will and strength of intention drive the intensity of this process. Through reliving Jesus' life with him, you have experienced lessons, meditations, and affirmations designed to help you remember this great journey home to the divine self. Taking this journey is your choice, and you alone must drive your experience of reconnection. You may invite masters and angels to assist you, but the choice to do the conscious work of release and reconnection is yours alone. You are seen as a master painter by God in every moment of your life, whether you are painting with pain or love. The power to create is a gift to us from God to use as we choose.

If you choose to create with love and conscious understanding, then state your will and intention strongly by saying the following steps of the divine model of awakening out loud.

1. *I willingly let go of personal chains binding me to others and this earthly life.*
2. *I willingly reconnect with my higher spirit-self and my own inner wisdom.*
3. *I willingly disconnect from conventional wisdom and follow my heart.*
4. *I willingly connect with the higher source of energy supporting the Earth and divine realms.*
5. *I willingly discover my higher purpose and create a plan of action.*
6. *I willingly live as a master in both the Earth and divine realms.*
7. *I willingly influence others to begin their own journeys home to the divine.*

Jesus learned firsthand how the power of the divine could change one life and touch the lives of millions on Earth. Jesus used the divine model of awakening with great commitment to reconnecting with his higher spirit-self and fulfilling his divine plan. He took the needed first step to realizing his divinity: a leap of faith. Step into the abyss of the unknown with a strong heart and you shall never walk alone.

Hear now as God explains the goal of the divine model of awakening:

Dear ones, you are brave journeyers, brave souls who came to this realm to explore. But at some point the journey ends, and it is time to find the road home. In this moment, the divine is reaching out to your brothers and sisters with more intensity than ever before in the history of the earthly experience. The clarion call has sounded, and I now call all home to me. Follow these keys, focus on the process of remembrance, for there is a grand reason for roadmaps surfacing in your world at this moment in time.

Jesus, following the divine model, reached a state of energetic grace and awareness of his inherent divinity and role in both the earthly and divine realms. Over time during his earthly existence, he shifted his awareness higher until his body became a blueprint for what is possible in living as an instrument of God. My dear friends, you can achieve all that Jesus did and more. You can achieve the same connection with your divinity and inner wisdom. You can touch others with the grace of God. Jesus, through his own experience, opened up new horizons for humanity. The possibilities of living heaven upon Earth now are endless, through the power of Jesus then and through your own creative power today.

Why are the keys to living a life of greater possibilities entering your world now? As divine beings, we create wonderful realms of experience for ourselves to learn and grow within. The beings of this beautiful earthly realm are now ready to shift into their divine consciousness. Jesus began this process two thousand years ago to show you how. Remember how grace is a natural part of your being, and you remember how easy it is to do this. Break free from the shackles of your human existence and reclaim your divine wisdom now.

Let the fear go and remember who you are with an open heart. Each step you take is toward a larger goal, but each step is in a moment of time. In that small step, concentrate on what is important. Knowing yourself fully and rising above the veil of shame and doubt are important to all of us. Be the master of this world and have the courage to look beyond the ordinary. Look for the signposts, the messages, the keys of remembrance that will guide you back to your higher spirit-self. Most of all, enjoy this journey, for that moment of awakening is exquisite.

Walking the Path of Christ

"Listen to me! I tell you I saw him here with my own eyes," the heavyset man told the disciples, pointing to the road in front of them. "He spoke to me and told me to always follow the path of truth. I felt lost and afraid upon the road, and I thought that I heard a sound from the bushes. When I turned around, he was there. It was dark, but he appeared like the day. It seemed like the sun was shining upon him even though the land around him was in darkness."

The disciples looked at each other. The boldest among them spoke first.

"This is the fourth sighting of the Lord that we have heard of," he said quietly. "Two by the tomb, one in the courtyard, and now along the road. I do not know what to make of this. Let us return to the house and decide what to do next."

Back at the house, a few of the men paced the room, while others sat despondently.

"If only the Lord were here, he would know what to do," a young disciple said quietly to himself.

Another disciple across the room stood up angrily, and yelled, "Jesus is not here. He died on the cross. A dead man does not disappear from a tomb or appear as alive to others. I do not believe any of this nonsense. He is gone, and this nonsense must stop."

Just then a bright light began to fill the room. It started in the center of the room as a bright star and continued to expand. The men all turned toward the light, jaws hanging, looks of disbelief upon their faces. The light continued to grow and took shape as a large oval. Then from this massive light, a body, a man of light appeared. The metamorphosis continued until standing before the disciples was their master, Jesus.

Smiling warmly, he said, "And what do you believe when you see me standing here before you? Must you see the brilliance of my garment to know the truth of my existence?"

All of the disciples dropped to their knees. The strongest-willed among them spoke first.

"My Lord, you have come to show us all that you do live. But how is that so? I saw your dead body upon the cross, and yet now it is gone. Tell me, master, for I do not understand how this is so," said the disciple, reaching his hand up to Jesus.

"Oh, my dear friends, do you not know a miracle when one stands before you?" Jesus asked. "I am the risen Christ, for I am in my father's house now. I come to you from this place of mastery and light. When I lived among you, I had the same body as you. But when I returned home to my father's house, I took it all with me."

The disciples looked questioningly at each other. During his life they often didn't understand Jesus, and this perplexity continued into his afterlife.

Jesus laughed and said, "What is this flesh upon your body but light? What are these bones but light? You eat and drink to make your body move so that you may do God's work. But what is this body but a divine creation here to do God's bidding? And when your earthly work is done, why should the body not return to the father's house? The father created it and it shall return to the father."

Jesus raised his hands to face the perplexed disciples. His hands appeared solid, but the men could see through them to the wall behind the master. Some took a step back from the Lord.

"When I say I love you, I am love in that moment. And I say to you, I love you all. See now what love is," said Jesus, as a misty pink light began flowing from his hands and eyes, surrounding and filling the entire room.

At first frightened by the light, the men slowly sat down on the floor as the love filled their beings. Many lay down upon the ground and promptly fell asleep. Soon the strong-willed disciple was the only man left sitting up awake.

Jesus slowly joined him on the floor. The disciple looked upon the master in front of him with great love and admiration.

Jesus placed his hand upon the disciple's and said, "And I feel the same for you, my dear friend. But I must leave you now, for my home is with my father now. But I am not so far away. I am only a thought, a breath, a heartbeat away, for I am always here," he said, placing his hand upon the man's chest, "deep within your heart."

Tears streamed down the disciple's cheeks. "Take me with you, master. I do not want to go on without you."

Smiling, Jesus placed his hand upon the man's shoulder. "When you leave this place tonight, I leave with you. When you reach out to another man in pain, I reach with you. When you tell others of the glories of God's kingdom, I tell with you. Ask and I shall be by your side always. I may not be there for you to see with your eyes, but I am always within your heart. Remember this always, and teach others how to find me."

As the disciple watched, Jesus' shape became blurry. Slowly, the image of his body faded into the oval, shrinking until only the star shone in the room. As quickly as the light had come, it now disappeared.

During his time on Earth, Jesus taught those he met to see God in everyone and everything. His belief in the power of God touched broken hearts and healed them into wholeness. Jesus' gift to us was his life, his example of letting God lead you, hold you, guide you, and lift you up to the light of day. His love for humanity is immense, and he gently sings our song in the quiet moments of our lives. When we listen closely, we can hear the words and remember them as our own.

A Love Song for Humanity

The light of God touches us every morning, in the quiet still hours of the day.

In the stillness, we feel God as an old friend.

"Yes, I am with you," he whispers when we place a blanket over a sleeping child.

"I am here," he says when we notice the sun kissing the petals of a flower growing unexpectedly in the desert sand.

"Take my hand," he says when we are afraid to cross the river alone.

"I am God," he sings joyfully when we feel him in our midst.

When anger strikes us down, when pain stops us in our path, when fear closes the door ahead of us, God is there.

"I am," God says, "always."

11

Jesus Reveals His True Place in Our World

WHEN the Apostle Paul spoke of the second coming of Christ, did he mean it literally or figuratively?

Since Jesus' death two thousand years ago, he has continued to touch the hearts of millions through the Gospels in the Bible; through ministers, pastors, and priests preaching the word of God; through congregants worshiping him in churches; and through seekers looking within to know Spirit on a deeper level. During his life on Earth, Jesus taught many along the path. Some, like Paul, were not counted among his original twelve disciples, but they played a great role in continuing to bring forth the word of God to the world after Jesus completed his divine plan on Earth.

Paul was touched by the love of Christ in a very ordinary place: in the darkness along the side of a road. He was tired and thirsty. He left the group he had been traveling with all day to rest in the quiet stillness behind some bushes. He lay his weary head down upon the ground and was overcome by sleep. As the night wore on, he awoke with a start, not fully aware of what had disturbed his sleep.

Looking up, he saw Jesus before him, awash in a brilliant white light.

"Be not afraid, for as I came to you in life, I come to you as a friend in death," he told Paul.

Now upon his knees, Paul begged Jesus for forgiveness. He had heard of the horrible things that occurred to Jesus during his final days on Earth but did not go to help him.

"Fear not, my friend, for all that occurred was within God's plan," Jesus said to him gently. "I bear no ill will toward you, my friend. But I do bring you a message from God. You have been chosen to carry on my work by bringing forth the good news of God. Your skills as a scribe are needed, as this will be recorded for all of humanity, all of the world, to read long after you are gone. Be ready, my friend, for these words will come to you like sweet nectar from a flower. They will flow sweetly, without reserve, for all to see and believe."

Paul stood up and held his arms out to Christ. "You can use me, dear master, and let me do now what I did not do then. Let me bring forth the good news of God and learn to live as you did."

"And so it shall be," Jesus said, slowly disappearing into the darkness.

Like Paul, we yearn for the glance of God in our lives. We yearn for the call of God to come to us, clearly and boldly, reminding us of our divine work on Earth. We yearn for the touch of Christ upon our shoulder, gently guiding and encouraging us to reveal our inner greatness.

In announcing the second coming of Christ, Paul reminds us of the importance of allowing the light of Christ to shine through us. As sacred vessels of God, we too act as Jesus did in illuminating the world with God's light. In remembering our sacred plan with God, Christ returns to work through us in our everyday life. Christ returns to Earth through us, and we return to our divine selves through him. In this great exchange, we each become the living Christ on Earth.

Breaking Down the Walls of Separation

Paul strongly felt that Jesus would return soon, ushering in a time of great peace and love. He felt so close to the energy of Christ by doing God's work upon Earth. What he didn't realize was that Christ was working through him, continuing his great work by supporting Paul's experiences on Earth in teaching others about the wonders of a loving God. All great prophets before Jesus and after Paul have been supported in the same way, bringing the same messages of hope, faith, and love to guide humanity if they so choose. Paul felt the return of Christ so strongly because it was occurring within him and through him.

And it is the same for us. We all hold within us a piece of heaven coexisting with our human experience of separation from God. Our experience of separation acts like a barrier, keeping us from knowing our true divine selves. When we die, we automatically break down the barriers of separation and reunite with our divine self. The divine model of awakening teaches us how to break down these walls without death and welcome the divine into our consciousness while in life.

This great shift to a higher level of conscious understanding is already occurring. Many of us are tapping into our own divine stream of wisdom and exploring and performing our divine plans now. Mastery qualities of love, compassion, forgiveness, and personal responsibility are flowing gracefully into our world, and many of us are pulling from this divine power to transform our own lives and the lives of others. Many of us are laying down our swords of pain, releasing old burdens, and reaching deep into our inner realms to remember our inherent divinity. Through this conscious refocusing on divine inner wisdom and acceptance of divine love, Christ is living through our hearts right now.

Hear now as Jesus explains how he will usher in a great time of peace, growth, love, and understanding:

My dear friends, the reunification with my higher spirit-self was a glorious journey and one that is not limited to my experience alone. You, dear ones, are capable of achieving all that I did. I am not above you but only an example for you to follow. Just as a master teaches his disciple, you too may learn from my journey and apply it to your own unique path.

These divine roads have led me home, but I still exist in your world through your remembrance of me. Each time you pray to me, commune with my spirit, and seek guidance on your own path, you are reaching out to me and bringing a tangible piece of me into this world. You embrace me with your physical energy and bring into form my teachings. By practicing the lessons I have learned during my journey, you bring into form my essence of peace and love, for I truly do represent the love of the divine for you.

You bring into form my Christlike attributes in yourself when you forgive another, let go of old pain, search for the truth, and live above the mundane aspects of the everyday world. Hear me closely now as I say to you that there is also a man in me who desires to share this journey again with you as master and disciple. My dear students of life, all is possible in the divine realm, and I desire to return to be with you once again, not in physical body but in spirit, guiding you, loving you, carrying your burdens, and allowing you to become a master in your own right.

Just as you continue your journey to completion, I too must finish my journey as it is written in my divine plan with God. I will be one among you again, one in the heart of humanity. Through your trusting hearts, your strong intentions, and your belief in life eternal, I return in those moments and lovingly restore peace on Earth. In these moments of connection, heaven shall open to you, and you again will see that you are not separate from God.

I exist only a breath away from you now. I am here to prepare you for the coming of peace, for things will change greatly as more people release the veils of separation and allow the light of God to shine forth from their being. We can prepare ourselves for the new world to be.

Things are changing greatly in the world around you. We have always known people who could remember their inner link to God, but at no time in history have all people been able to readily connect with the divine for guidance and communication. The time is ripe, as is the environment around you. The divine world coexists with you much as the Internet and phones use the same lines for communication: phones use certain frequencies for communication, while the Internet uses other frequencies within the same line. These two forms of communication exist simultaneously in one receiver/ sender line.

It is the same with us. You exist on a denser, lower frequency. We exist right within your world on a higher frequency. If you take away the barrier of separation, you can see us in your world. The barrier acts as a screen, keeping out the higher vibrations and allowing you to perceive yourself as having a separate experience from the divine. Truly, you are not, for we are always here with you.

As more people break down the barrier between their human selves and divine selves, more divine energy will filter through, and you will begin to perceive the divine world around you. You will begin to perceive your higher spirit-self, your angels, your guides, and other ascended beings around you. You will perceive light in a new way, for light energy is the lifeblood of our existence. Light is abundant and great, full of flowing, moving energy that can be shaped to create incredible worlds of great depth. Believe me when I say to you that light energy is the basis of this all. Light moves quickly, changes quickly. When this barrier breaks down, things will change quickly. The breaking down of barriers is a joyous, wondrous event, a time of reunification of self. You truly will become more Christlike, for you will connect back into that part of you which is greater than your existence now.

The Illumination of Heaven's Light

Heaven's light illuminates our universe, which seems to have been created just for us. It perfectly fulfills all of our needs for food, shelter, love, and creativity. We have tried to master this world by building upon it, tearing it down, moving it, and even making our own new world out in space. All of this experience, this creativity unbounded, is valid in this world, for we are here to push the limits of our existence until we remember that we are truly limitless. We are here to allow heaven's light to change how we perceive our earthly life.

What do you see when you hold your hand in front of you? Do you see flesh and blood, an organic expression of the divine? Do you see calluses, hands worn from labor and strife? Do you see a simple instrument for reaching out to others? Or do you see nothing at all, for your own hand is an unwelcome stranger in your life?

In this world, great masters in human form can run astray from the divine flock. It is quite easy to forget your greatness and see yourself as unworthy of love or even a handshake. You may see yourself as ugly, unrefined, or uninteresting. Others may have told you the same. You may carry these burdens in your being, and your physical body may begin to show the mis-perceptions you are laboring under. You may have ailments or injuries that attest to the lack of self-worth you feel. You are laboring under many misperceptions based upon a world of lim-itations. But at the heart of your essence, you are greater than that little person you portray yourself to be. Remembering that truth, trusting that truth, and believing that truth will truly set you free from your limited existence and allow heaven's light to illuminate your new path.

Hear now as Mother Mary explains how to let down your guard to seeing heaven's light around you:

Dear ones, my heart is close to yours now. I know how this world can seem so big, so real, so insurmountable. Jesus, my dear son on Earth, looked life's challenge square in the face and said, "Yes, I can. Yes, I can be larger than the smallest ideas I have about myself. Yes, I can break out of old familial molds that bind my heart and my dreams. Yes, I can live a life helping others to see the greatness within themselves. Yes, I can do all of this despite what others may think of me. Some may see me as uneducated. Some may think me too brash. Some may not like the color of my skin or the clothes I wear. Some may turn away at the sight of me. But I care not, for I am always in my father's house. My heavenly home exists in the here and now, right before you and me. I am always loved, whether I hear it with my physical ears or my inner ears. I am love eternal, always abundant, always flowing, always available to all and the many."

Let not your fears ever lead you to believe otherwise. This great abundant God of the universe is a loving being, full of care, understanding, and compassion. You are made from the same cloth. You hold all of this within you. Let it see the light of day. Know that you are a master in your own right, on the path to coexisting in the divine and earthly realms. Know who you are always: a divine being having a human experience. Let not the mud of the experience cover up your true essence. Let the fear lie below you as you soar above the clouds.

I know this world for I have been in this world. Let me help you carry your burden. Give your pain to me, and allow me to give you the wisdom that is rightfully yours. Claim it now and walk beside Jesus in peace when he reaches out to lead you through this veil of illusion.

Heaven's light is the light of Christ, and in this bright light of truth, you cannot be any less than who you are. God sees you as whole and perfect, but only you can choose to see yourself in the same light. Through our life experiences, we can exist in varying degrees of light. On one end of the spectrum lies darkness, where our thoughts hold no light of truth and from which we can commit the basest actions. In the middle, in the gray zone of illumination, we operate on a low level where we may see glimpses of truth, but we find it difficult to hold our actions up to the light and examine the motives for our behavior. On the other end of the spectrum lies the light, full and abundant, guiding our actions from a place of truth, love, acceptance, and peace. All of the light, from the fullness to the absence of light, is heaven's light. All of our experiences, based on the spectrum of lightness to darkness, are within heaven's light. Only when we choose to consciously live in heaven's light do we allow the light of Christ to govern and illuminate all of our actions.

Hear now as Jesus explains how to consciously choose heaven's light:

My beloved ones, I too have lived many experiences, accumulating many keys, and discovering many things about this universe and myself. You may see me as above you, but I have grown into who I am just as you seek to do too. I am who I am because of my belief, faith, perseverance, and pure joy— I do this because I love to learn and grow.

Your mastery lies deep within you, waiting for you to unlock the mysteries, the desires, the fulfillment of your destiny. Whether you are here to explore or serve others through performing a divine role, you are a master. This mastery accumulates over time, and as you tap into it while on Earth, you automatically access it with ease. Let your fears go and tap into the inner knowledge that is uniquely your own. When you tap into your greatness, you tap into the greatness of heaven's light.

When you acknowledge this love of experience, you accept heaven's light in your world. Heaven's light makes this experience possible, for without the light, there would not be any energy to fuel your world. When you remember your link with heaven's light, you access your inherent power. The darkness is just an absence of light, a choice not to behave within the illumination of your true essence. Behavior in the darkness may be judged by others as evil, but your true essence is not evil. In the darkness, you are just laboring under the illusion of no illumination or truth about the outcome of your actions. Darkness is a form of separation from heaven's light. Grayness, the midpoint between light and dark, is another form of separation. During life, we all choose points of separation and the level of light we operate under. When you choose heaven's light to illuminate your actions and behavior, you choose to live as I did as a vessel of God. Heaven's light will then illuminate your world and touch others. Look within, and you will find the same traits for greatness, for we are made from the same cloth.

The Power of Love's Light

When Jesus lived on Earth, he spoke of love and light. He told people that he loved them for who they were and forgave their sins. He showed compassion for the meek, the rich, and those who had forgotten their inner temple of God. He was a reminder to us all of the power of love's light.

Along the spectrum of lightness to darkness, love's light exists at every point, waiting to change hearts from pain and fear to love and truth. Love's light illuminates our choices, giving us the opportunity to choose growth and reconnection with Spirit in every experience. In the moment a choice is made, love's light can be used to illuminate the options. This light comes from remembering our divine connection and our ability to shift our focus from pain to love at any time. When we use love to govern our choices, we are allowing love's light, our Christ light, to shine forth. Jesus was a bringer of love's light, a living example of love in action.

Hear now as God explains how we use our heart of love:

Dear ones, it is with great love and affection that I tell you about the relationship between light and love in your world. We as divine beings are made up of love: love for humanity, love for the human condition, love for ourselves—for when I love you, I love myself. As divine beings, we are not capable of harm—we are benign beings. In the fullness of heaven's light in the divine realm, divine beings only experience love. Because we exist completely in this light of abundance, we extend the soul of our higher spirit-selves into human selves in the earthly realm. Here in this illusionary realm that I created using a wider spectrum of lightness and darkness, we may experience life in ways that are different from our true state of abundance. Here on Earth, you know what it is like to be limited, and you know what it is like to feel pain. Your experiences add to our general holding of knowledge and from this, we continue to grow and evolve into a greater understanding of sentient beings.

When you say, "I love you," you are acknowledging your essence. When you allow love to guide your choices, you are consciously choosing to operate from a higher level of being. On this level, you are allowing your divine wisdom to govern your actions, and it is in this light of truth that you break down barriers to knowing your divine heart in all moments. You are no longer just a human being. You become a divine being in human form experiencing reconnection with the light of love. When you choose to live completely in the light of love, heaven's light illuminates all of your thoughts, feelings, and actions. You have reached a state of enlightenment, and your world shines brightly for all to see.

This is the world I seek in all of you. This is the world I manifest for you. This is the world of light that allows creation to exist on Earth as it does in heaven. In the light, in abundance, is where you will embrace the God of your heart again. From light to light, you are created, and so shall you return to the divine as light.

Love's light, the light of Christ, exists in all of us when we show a desire to learn, grow, change, and embrace the truth of our existence. We live in love's light as the beloved sons and daughters of God, just like Jewsus. We are created through the love of God, just like Jesus. We are born into this world to achieve greatness, just like Jesus. We have a divine plan to explore and perform to serve ourselves and others, just like Jesus. We will return to God in a glorious moment of unification with our essence, just like Jesus. We are made from light, and we shall return to the light, just like Jesus.

We are love's light. We are living miracles. The following parable reminds us of the miracle of our existence and the destiny we all must fulfill during our time on Earth.

The Light of the Child

"Let me help him," the man said as he bent over the small child, crying in the basket.

Gently, he picked up the swaddled babe in his arms, rocking him slowly back and forth. The mother looked on in love as this kind man soothed her only son. As the child's eyes slowly closed, the man placed him back in his crib.

Putting her finger over her mouth, the woman motioned for the man to join her outside on the porch. Together they sat on the swing and looked up at the brilliant night sky. The stars were blazing that night, and a gentle breeze cooled their bare feet.

"He is amazing," the man whispered. "I didn't believe it when I spoke to you on the phone, but seeing him in person has changed my mind."

"My brother, you do doubt much until you see it with your own eyes," his sister chided him, gently rapping him on the arm.

"No doubt here," he replied. "I now know what Jesus meant when he said that a piece of him exists in us all. Just holding him makes me want to be a better person. More loving, more understanding."

He stopped and smiled at his sister. "No doubt here. He's just like the sacred one. He inspires me to be more than I am."

Living in the Light

Each of us is here to explore the mysteries of existence, to discover the hidden jewels that lie beneath the surface of everyday life. It is in this great realm of the unknown that we begin to discover the vastness of our being and just why we are truly here. Jesus took this journey of the unknown so that he could lead by example. Just as he led during his physical life on Earth, he continues to lead from his life eternal.

Like the book of Jesus' life, you will create your own record, your own diary of experiences that will explain your existence. You too will lead a life worthy of dissection by others for keys of mastery. Just as Jesus is a divine master, you are a master in your own right.

Hear now as God blesses you upon your journey of the heart:

Beloved ones, you are so amazing in all that you do. You came to Earth, great journeyers, to discover and learn more about yourself in a situation of limitation. We have given you many clues for mastering the game, but now you must take these keys and use them to unlock the door between the earthly and divine realms.

This is my plan for you and this universe: Master the game now for the game is coming to a new level. In this new level, you will experience life in a whole new way, without limitations. In this higher realm of existence, you will learn to reunite the peace of your higher spirit-self with your human self. You will have greater opportunities to let go of old pain and gain knowledge. You will know once again that you are a divine being.

My dear ones, my creations of love, it is all here before you. Know my love for you. Know how closely I stand beside you as you travel through this life. Know that I am always here for each and every one of you.

If there is one thing that you should take from this divine model of awakening, let it be this: I love you. And therein lies your strength.